Writers of Wales

EDITORS

MEIC STEPHENS   R. BRINLEY JONES

DANNIE ABSE

Tony Curtis

DANNIE
ABSE

*University of Wales Press
on behalf of the Welsh Arts Council*

1985

Dannie Abse is one of the two most widely read and respected living poets of Wales. He, like R. S. Thomas, was born in Cardiff; unlike Thomas he has based his life outside Wales, in London, and travels regularly between his house in Golders Green and his house in Ogmore-by-Sea (where, he says, he was conceived). He is by profession a doctor and that fact is as central to his work as the priesthood has been to R. S. Thomas. By birth a Jew, Dannie Abse's inclination has always been unorthodox and questioning. He is fascinated by the power of religion, but suspicious of dogmas and the exclusive assumptions of priesthoods. While Thomas in the North has appeared a private, at times remote figure, Abse, the South Walian, has been determinedly a public figure. His work, particularly the poems, autobiographical and critical writing, frequently explores personal feeling and experiences. To a large extent one reads the books and meets the man.

He has said:

Certainly my poems relate, in hidden narrative my true biography.

1

but there are also several books of direct and of fictional autobiography to consider. What is clear is that out of his poetry and prose works a picture emerges of a singular life and a significant writer.

Peter Porter, reviewing the COLLECTED POEMS, locates the particular quality of this writing.

Abse's right to ask unanswerable questions about life and death comes from his willingness to keep his attention fixed on all that is visible and comprehensible in daily existence.

   There is a persistent note of humanism throughout his poetry which is never wishful thinking or mere scepticism . . . His litanies are mostly questions and it is a measure of his skill as a poet that he manages to make them expansive and memorable . . .

The circumstances of his life are often at the centre of his writing, but recording them is seldom the sole purpose of his work. Talking of the important lessons he learnt from reading and re-reading Rainer Maria Rilke, he says:

What I could have learnt and should have learnt from Rilke was the value of experience in making a poem. That I was to learn later when I began to believe poems should not begin with ideas but rather spring from true or imagined experience.
   (The Gwyn Jones Annual Lecture, 1984)

The true *and* imagined experiences of his life have fuelled a prolific and varied body of writing. Reading Dannie Abse we learn a lot about life, and a lot about writing.

Dannie Abse was born in 1923 in Cardiff, in a 'smoky house' in Whitchurch Road. In the first

2

years of his life the family moved frequently from one rented house to another. As a house reached the point at which it needed re-decorating, the tenants would move on. A number of addresses in Albany Road and Sandringham Road led eventually to a newer, more comfortable semi-detached in Windermere Avenue, a short walk from the pleasant acres of Roath Park, in the suburbs of the city.

Dannie was the youngest of four children: he had a sister, Huldah, and two brothers. Wilfred now practises medicine in the U.S.A., and Leo is the long-serving Labour Party Member of Parliament for Torfaen (formerly the Pontypool seat) particularly noted for his divorce reform work. Dannie's earliest ambitions were 'to play football for Cardiff City, rugby for Wales, cricket for Glamorgan.'

At Marlborough Road Elementary School his teachers included one 'Inky' Williams, who also stood on the terraces at Ninian Park and swore passionately at the City's football team; and George Thomas, who was to enter Parliament and become Secretary of State for Wales. Dannie also attended Chedar at the Windsor Place Synagogue where he struggled to pronounce and understand Hebrew, but was fascinated by the Old Testament stories told in English. At his secondary school, St. Illtyd's College, he was taught by the Christian Brothers. As the only Jewish boy at the school he was a comparatively detached observer of the dogmatic Christianity there; though he was once admonished for arguing in a debate against marriage as an institution.

3

He played rugby for the school, once breaking his collar-bone in a match. Abse, the schoolboy patient, announced in Casualty:

I'm going to be a medical student.
(A POET IN THE FAMILY)

Wilfred was the model for his young brother in this respect. He had studied medicine at Cardiff University College, King's College, London and later at Westminster Hospital. Wilfred had said that Westminster was, 'The best hospital in the world,' and Dannie's name had been put down for a place when he was thirteen. This fact is less remarkable when one learns that two of his uncles were doctors and that five of his cousins were also to enter the profession.

Dannie's father managed and part-owned a cinema in Aberdare. He was a man expressive in his moods.

When he was gay he told jokes; when moodily sad he would take down his violin and, with eyes closed like a lover, play Kreisler's 'Humoresque' until he became, for all the grey and green world of Wales, a model for Chagall.
(A POET IN THE FAMILY)

His mother was fluent in Hebrew and Welsh and could recite lengthy extracts from poems such as Longfellow's 'Hiawatha'. This, at times, she did to the captive audience in her house.

The intellectual energies of Wilfred and Leo ensured that Dannie Abse was

exposed to the adult dialogue of the thirties—to the dialogue
between Sigmund Freud and Karl Marx.

(A POET IN THE FAMILY)

His sister, Huldah, played the popular hits of the
day on the radiogram and, when he was of an
age, she rolled back the carpet and taught him
to dance. So the Abse household was a bustling,
wordy, stimulating place in which to grow and
Dannie's childhood and adolescence in Cardiff
were to provide the impulse for much of his later
writing. His early models were the young martyrs
of The Spanish Civil War—Cornford, Fox,
Caudwell—the dead writers whose work he read
in Leo's copies of LEFT REVIEW.

In his time at Cardiff University College he met
John Stuart Williams and Bernice Rubens, the
poet and novelist respectively, both of whom
would find success in later years. For Dannie
Abse the idea of writing had taken root by then.
The arguments and books of his brothers; the
songs and speeches of the late thirties; Churchill's
broadcast wartime speeches—there was a swirl of
language around Dannie Abse.

In A POET IN THE FAMILY he recalls how his father
insisted that they listen to Ezra Pound in his
propaganda broadcasts for the Italian fascists.
Perhaps, he reasoned, out of the man's rantings
one might glean intimations of how the war was
really going. These were the years of rhetoric,
used for both good and evil purposes. A Jewish
family with two sons conscripted *had* to take
notice.

5

The Abses were and are proudly Jewish and proudly Welsh. Dannie's father came from Bridgend and his mother's family were from the small valley town of Ystalyfera, north of Swansea.

When my grandfather, in 1887, was invited to preach in the chapel at Ystalyfera, when he uttered translated Hebrew rhetoric of this kind, David spoke to Dafydd, and the Nonconformist congregation found neither the substance nor the manner of his sermon alien.
(The Gwyn Jones Annual Lecture, 1984)

Dannie Abse is then the natural heir to two traditions of voicing human needs. But there is more to take account of than that. This writer will not simply fit into a predictable scheme of things.

In the recent Gwyn Jones Annual Lecture, entitled 'Under the Influence of', Dannie Abse is most anxious to exclude himself from an over-view of Anglo-Welsh literature that is based on generalisations concerning the language, the 'seepage' from the old tongue into contemporary English, and the Biblical rhetoric that springs most forcefully from the Nonconformist tradition in Wales. The influences that determined him as a writer are more complex. They can be traced through the prose works over thirty years, from ASH ON A YOUNG MAN'S SLEEVE to A STRONG DOSE OF MYSELF, as well as in the poems themselves. Some are obvious in the craft of the poems (too obvious by far in the early work) others become more fully subsumed into the poet's art.

What Dannie Abse learns, and it is this for which

we value him most, is to be open to experience and the feelings that call forth the need for poetry. The very first poem in the COLLECTED POEMS is 'The uninvited', the only one he wishes to preserve from 1946 and his first collection. That poem was stimulated by an idea in Rilke's correspondence with Kappus in 1904. When we are open to important moments of sorrow, then, Rilke says, *our future sets foot in us*, our destiny begins and *we have been changed as a house is changed into which a guest has entered.*

Dannie Abse is an accessible, welcoming writer. His work draws us in as readers, but then invariably we find ourselves in a place much stranger than we had expected—odd, mysterious, even threatening. As the young boy in ASH ON A YOUNG MAN'S SLEEVE discovers the complex world outside his own happy childhood and grows to take his place in it, so the mature writer's work encourages growth in the sensibility of his reader; it demands that an empathy should exist between those who share the human condition.

ASH ON A YOUNG MAN'S SLEEVE was written when Dannie Abse was in his late twenties, and first published in 1954. He had by then published two collections of poems and was beginning to attract an audience as a poet. Hutchinsons, who accepted his first collection in 1946 when he was still a medical student, undoubtedly encouraged their rising young poet to consolidate his position with a novel.

The book that Dannie Abse wrote is usually listed as a novel, often prefixed by the qualification 'autobiographical'. However, the Corgi edition carries the disclaimer, *The author wishes to emphasise that this book is not autobiographical, for events and characters have been thoroughly fictionalised.* No doubt this served a legal purpose as much as an emotional one. In any case only the most gullible reader accepts anyone's autobiography as history. One may use the names, characters, family relationships, neighbourhoods of one's past, making constant reference to authentic historical events, and still be creating fiction.

Writing always involves editing. Dannie Abse immediately acknowledges that in his 1983 collection of prose A STRONG DOSE OF MYSELF. Talking of Edwin Muir's autobiography, he says:

Yet autobiography itself is a kind of fiction.

and argues, this time in response to William Carlos Williams,

. . . the autobiographer courageously destroys his past experiences by naming them . . . an autobiography with all its approximate resemblances, buries the real life of the autobiographer. The life that was real becomes extinct.

Out of the ashes of that 'real life' rises the phoenix that is made new—a more mythical, stronger beast by far—fiction,

Autobiography in the hands of such poets as Carlos Williams and Edwin Muir need not be adjacent to literature, it can be literature itself.

8

The author of ASH ON A YOUNG MAN'S SLEEVE does not need to labour the point, for his first work of fiction in this vein is a classic of its kind.

However, it may not instantly win the reader's admiration. In its opening pages, and at some other points in its narration, the writing seems to chase the afterglow of the recently-dead Dylan Thomas.

I was ten years high and I lived in South Wales

And indeed the capital city of Cardiff seems to have its own Cwmdonkin Park.

In the Park it said PLEASE KEEP OFF THE GRASS and DOGS ALLOWED ONLY ON A LEASH. I kicked the notices over. In the distance the park-keeper stabbed with his little iron spear, cigarette cartons, pieces of newspaper and other rubbish. Old men were playing bowls over the West Side. Young men were taking off their tigerish blazers to play tennis on the red gravel court. Lol, the idiot boy, was fishing with a net for tiddlers in the brook whilst another lad repeatedly banged the chained metal cup against the fountain for no reason.

The park-keeper *with his stick that picked up leaves*, the tigerish shapes, the chain cup and the idiot boy are all born of Dylan's work, as is the following

Keith and I used to play hide-and-seek in the nearby church-yard, our laughter resounding all loveliness amongst the sombre stone angels.

There are also echoes of Richard Llewellyn in the sentimentality

Oh, sing my beautiful, Sospan Fach, Cwm Rhondda.
They would sing . . .

and in the use of inversion as a means to create
'Welshness'

Lovely it was . . .

These influences, however indirect, are hardly
surprising. Llewellyn's How GREEN WAS MY VALLEY,
first published in 1938, had been a best-selling
novel during the war years and was moving
towards its fortieth printing as ASH ON A YOUNG
MAN'S SLEEVE appeared. For many readers outside Wales our small country was characterised,
if at all, in Llewellyn's terms.

Dylan Thomas's death in 1953 was, remarkably
for a poet, front-page news. Dylan, wild, eloquent
and doomed, left a powerful legacy for literary
Welshmen to inherit. It would have been surprising indeed if the young Abse had not been
tempted to emulate two such successful writers
from Wales, especially the charismatic Dylan
whom his brother Leo had actually drunk with

Oh, it was fairy tales ago, in days of butterflies and blue-
bottles, in nights when the cool dark skies gave me hollyhock,
and the heatwave in the summer of 1934, and the Brighton
Trunk Mystery. It was holidays of hide-and-seek, in the
churchyard of gold struck graves and sunwater filtering
through the curtains of drowned furnished rooms. It was sun
right down to my red buried heart and laughing and crying,
singing and fighting, under the endless blue, July heaven.

Of his first publication, the collection of poems
AFTER EVERY GREEN THING, Dannie Abse has said

Yes, they are immature. I was immature. I caught like an infection, the neo-romantic fashionable mode of the time.

What is remarkable though is the way in which his strength as a prose writer develops rapidly as Ash on A Young Man's Sleeve progresses. It is as if he emerges from a cocooned style flexing his own wings to take his own route. One senses the writer's growing recognition that his material is strong enough and sufficiently distinct from that of Thomas and Llewellyn to lead him to his own style and narrative strategies

for in writing an autobiography a man may find one more pathway towards self-revelation.

Dannie Abse talks directly of this process in the Essay 'A Voice of my Own', included in A Strong Dose of Myself.

When I look back at my earliest published work of the late 1940's I discern not only the then fashionable manner of neo-romanticism, but the unpremeditated influences, too dominant, of Dylan Thomas and Rainer Maria Rilke. Whatever individual voice I owned had to make itself heard above such noisy echoes. It seems to me now, what is probably obvious to everybody else, that a poet's progress towards discovering his own voice is marked by the shuffling off of all discernible individual influences.

Whereas Llewellyn sought to romanticise the collective experiences of a nation stretched on the rack of the Industrial Revolution, and Thomas gazed sadly, angrily out from the loud cave of himself, Dannie Abse's prose is fuelled by an abiding fascination with the circumstances of his family life, particularly in his formative years. Whilst Dylan's stories are the product of a self-centred child focussing himself in 'an ugly, lovely town', Dannie Abse's writing works from the considerable interest of his immediate family as characters.

His two elder brothers influence the growing boy in a profound way: Wilfred, the medical student and future eminent psychiatrist, reports constantly on his day at the hospital; Leo, the future, flamboyant Member of Parliament for Pontypool, is an informed, angry, politicised young man finding his way in the troubled and confusing middle 1930s.

Leo came in, 'Any post?' He propped up the Daily Worker against the tea-pot and attacked his fried egg.
'Terrible,' he muttered from time to time, 'Terrible, terrible.'
'What is it?' Mother asked.
'Terrible, terrible.'

Dannie Abse's childhood is simply more interesting than most people's and though the insights, embarrassments and sadnesses of his early life have a familiar pattern, ASH ON A YOUNG MAN'S SLEEVE is structured in such a way that the personal experiences are heightened by the continuing and swelling sense of wider issues and momentous events in Europe. At ten, Dannie Abse already knew the 'Red Flag' and the Alphabet.

A stands for Armaments, the Capitalists' pride, B stands for Bolshie, the thorn in their side . . .

These political noises may be recounted tongue-in-cheek at the beginning of the book, but the references and the commitment intensifies as the story moves further into the decade. July 1934 and the forest fires in England are a suggestion of other disasters, other colours, of black smoke appearing in the blue-hot skies of Europe.

It was July 1934 and a heat-wave when the mercury jumped to eighty-three degrees in the shade, when fires started on the English heaths; and in the forest, terrible jaws of flame consumed the turf and the shrieking trees with their jagged yellow fangs. Even as Keith and I sunbathed at Barry Island, all day long elsewhere there was the great crashing of dead branches, and columns of black smoke sat in the windless blue-hot skies. Yes, that July began with the torture of burnt trees in halcyon English woods; Captain Roehm shot dead in Germany, Dr Dollfuss shot dead in Austria, and a man called Hitler screaming: 'I beat down the revolution before it had time to spring up. I gave the order to burn out the tumours. He who lifts his hand for a blow against the State must know that death is his punishment.' In the Reichstag, they sang the Horst Wessel song with tears staining their eyes. In England, the amazing July of drought. In San Francisco, a general strike that paralysed that city and there were bullets in the streets and men, ordinary men, with curious grey flesh dead in the stricken gutters. The noise fell over the world: 'Stormy Weather', 'Lazybones', 'Miss Otis Regrets', and Mussolini strutting through the Piazzo Esedra. Oswald Mosley posing on a lonely platform in London behind an immense red, white and blue Union Jack. 'We the English'—shouted Mosley—'we the English are being throttled and strangled by the greasy fingers of alien financiers.' And he was talking about Dad and Mam, Wilfred and Leo, me and Uncle Isidore.

Recollections of an essentially happy childhood are counterpointed by these wider references. As the boy grows up into an adolescent awareness of the world's complexity, the world beyond Cardiff itself moves inexorably towards the Second World War.

Dannie Abse writes with the certainty of someone whose life does appear to be exhibiting a pattern. One of the most notable features of this autobiographical novel is the way in which the author re-creates historical events strategically vital to the narrative. That which has become an established fictional strategy in the work of Mailer, E. L. Doctorow, D. M. Thomas and others is employed sparingly but with a fine touch by the younger Abse.

These passages of 'faction' are a successful projection of the author's imagination into others' lives. The realisation of other Jews' experiences in Europe—the Grynszpan assassination, the burning of the synagogues and the nightmare transformation at Cardiff station are especially effective.

In the last of these, Dannie Abse remembers waiting on the platform for his parents to return from London. There, the accumulated weight of his impressions of that 'low dishonest decade' create a horrifying vision of tragic parallels.

The mechanical voice of the loudspeaker floated disembodied across the station clock that had stopped long ago in the year 1933. The sinister German voice mingled with the Guards in black uniforms and the sorrowful Alsatian dogs cocked up their ears. The voice over the crackling loud-speaker shouted, 'All change at Auschwitz–Dachau.' The engine gave a shriek of pain and the dogs would not look. Near the Refreshment Room stood a hygenic-looking shed containing a few gas chambers, inside one of which a stray passenger now found himself.

The rest of the passengers sat in the train, their luggage on the rack of pain. These suitcases were labelled Munich, Berlin, Vienna, Madrid, Prague. When the engine gave its plaintive shriek in the still air, no passenger moved, no passenger spoke. They merely sat, the hook-nosed ones, gazing straight ahead, waiting for the train to move out. Not looking at the pictures lining the carriages. Neither that of Hitler addressing a huge crowd, nor aeroplanes over Barcelona, nor troops goose-marching through Austria. Nobody looked, nobody spoke, nobody waved a last farewell.

A Guard came and opened the door. 'All change!' he screamed. They changed into skeletons. Skeletons row after row sitting bolt upright in the carriages of Time.

The loudspeaker crackled again. The next train to arrive at platform two will be the London train. The engine pulled in.

'There they are,' said Uncle Bertie.

Leo bundled out of the train, mother and father after him, smiling.

Dannie Abse's acknowledgement of his Jewishness becomes more significant as this book develops. The pains and responsibilities which that fact carries will be a major consideration in his fourth collection of poems POEMS, GOLDERS GREEN, 1956–1961—I have in mind 'After the Release of Ezra Pound', 'Red Balloon' and 'Postmark'. As he made clear in interview for THE JEWISH QUARTERLY in 1964:

Auschwitz made me more of a Jew than ever Moses did.

In ASH ON A YOUNG MAN'S SLEEVE though, a more immediate consequence of the war is Keith's death in a German air-raid. While Phyllis the housekeeper takes shelter under the stairs, Keith stubbornly continues to play his mother's piano. His end is a bizarre echo of his mother's death at the beginning of the novel.

The death of Mrs Thomas—her piano lid *closed, a coffin of music*—and the unrealised grief and love that the author feels for Keith, his friend, serves to validate his emotional responses through the remainder of the book. That emotional involvement with others is the prime shaping force in the novel. In his juxtaposition of scenes and facts, the anecdotal and the documentary, Dannie Abse creates a compelling, impressionistic landscape of the Thirties.

The section woven around Leo's quoting of Gerard Manley Hopkins' 'Pied Beauty' is particularly effective. It opens with the youngest Abse climbing into bed with his parents one Saturday morning and asking the enormous questions of one growing into the real world of adults. Then, the section expands the Hopkins line, *Glory be to God for dappled things*, and develops a collage of experiences occurring on that one rainy day in 1934. The miner Alun and his young wife Gwennie (names suggested perhaps by Alun and Gweno Lewis?) climb the hills above their valley. As the rain begins to sweep over them, Alun considers the lure of England and the possibility of job security there. Back in Cardiff the Rev. Aaronowich leads his congregation in the synagogue and

16

Thousands of years of faith leaned with the men as they leaned—those exiled Jews whose roots were in the dangerous ghetto and in dismayed beauty.

After the service the young Abse takes a tram into town, rattling down Queen Street where

an ex-miner played an accordion, a tombstone in one of his lungs. The music soared plaintively, insistently, across the rainy street: give, give, give, give, give. The traffic lights changed to green—the orange reflection rubbed off the wet surface of the road and a blue-green smudge usurped its blurred place. And the traffic passed on, passed on. The rain, thin and delicate, lost from the damp sky, suddenly fell forever.

The realisation grows that things are varied, multiple, diverse, that the world is unified by inclusion, that the whole can, and has to include all things. That realisation is the root from which an individual matures. Believing in the world as 'dappled' is to affirm individual rights, uniqueness, and to stand against the political swing to fascism in Europe at that time.

It is significant that this belief is, from the very beginning, realised in a studied use of language, and specifically in poetry. Near the end of the book the teenage Abse is left on the beach at Ogmore while Keith goes riding with the compelling but inaccessible Henrietta Gregory. In the 'dog-chained growling sea' he has a vision.

of the vertical death of the drowned, of the white-haired prisoners in the sea, and those others who slept in the feathery fathoms below the watery grey and green eiderdown that was pulled back and fore by the two-time swell.

17

and later, lying back to dry on the beach

Something moved across the heart like a benediction. It is hard to explain. It would be easier to describe a colour no-one had ever seen.

Only I felt a great exultation and a holiness I never sensed before and have only experienced once since. I felt I was given the power to do enormous good. And that delusion stayed with me for the rest of the morning.

This need is most obviously expressed at the book's end with the author following his eldest brother Wilfred into medical school. But the passage is also significant in relation to poetry. A doctor works for life itself: a poet works to celebrate the 'dappled thing' of life. This novel's final pages not only secure one's sense of having followed a rite of passage, but also leave one convinced that Dannie Abse has a clear perspective on the world. On the one hand he works to postpone 'the death of leaves' and on the other hearing 'their untranslatable leaf-vocabulary' and wants to press those words into the service of his poetry. In ASH ON A YOUNG MAN'S SLEEVE and in all his serious writing Dannie Abse is unquestionably moral. His writing has insight and sympathy for those who suffer in the world.

The music soared plaintively, insistently, across the raining street: give, give, give, give, give.

SOME CORNER OF AN ENGLISH FIELD (1956) was Dannie Abse's first attempt to write a novel that was not strictly autobiographical. It appeared in a single edition and is now not easily available. The book is not listed in the front of the

18

COLLECTED POEMS, and many of his regular
readers may not be aware of it.

Taken as a second novel it is, admittedly, a
disappointment. But if one approaches the book
as, *de facto*, a writer's first extended fiction, then
one may find much more to commend.

The situation is an R.A.F. camp in England during the middle fifties with National Service in
full swing. The two medical officers serving there
are Andrew Henderson, the central character of
the book, and his superior, Tom Wood. Wood is
a tired man, ground down by the pettiness of
service life and the banality of the recruiting
centre:

*National Service boys homesick—suffering with boils or
blisters on their feet or scratching away at scabs maybe.*

He drinks and is careless both of his duties and
his wife.

Abse uses a variety of points of view in his narration, but the novel's main thrust comes from our
involvement with these two doctors. Henderson,
the younger man, is a naturally better practitioner, a more helpful, imaginative character.
He wins the respect of the men who come to
him and he wins the older man's wife. If there is
an identification to be made between the author
and any character, then that character must be
Henderson.

The novel is pushed towards a more complex
and interesting state, however, by the insights we

are given into Wood's character. He is drenched in lethargy—

She never demanded much from him now, except to irritate him about his rank and need for promotion. And she seemed content to flirt with his successive junior officers. There was no harm in that, even if she went to bed with them occasionally. It didn't matter to him on any deep level, though it wasn't something to be discussed openly. 'Let sleeping dogs lie,' he thought.

Henderson's affair with Sarah Wood is predictable but sufferable. Tom Wood is apparently numb and compliant, accepting that his life with Sarah is fixed, unyielding, with nowhere to run:

At one point they'd put their life on certain rails and it had gone down the track on its own accord to stop somewhere, here, in a dingy siding, to rust quietly away, come rain or shine.

It is a difficult task to dramatise the predicament of such a character. We, like Wood himself, have little to wait for except his death. In the fourth chapter, midway through the novel, Tom Wood attempts suicide. Feeling unmoved, and numb to the events and issues of his like, and in a state of depression, he stands on the river bridge considering the prospect of taking his own life.

Wood took from his pocket a penny. He could feel the body-warmth of his own life on the metal and he dropped it over the bridge. It cut open the surface of the water and vanished into the darkness leaving only a flurry of circular ripples moving away from an invisible centre. Nobody noticed. The coin would be the cold temperature of the water on the river-bed. You could disappear like that: a few ripples of emotion maybe, moving further and further away from a central grief, until they became indistinguishable, a shapeless forgotten alteration in somebody else's soul. Sarah would still be playing gramophone records probably in some London flat and maybe think of him once a year like a duty. The untranslatable fluid of self-pity filtered behind his eyes. Now he was only a hole in the air. Afterwards he'd be a hole in the ground. Nobody would notice the difference.

Though appearing to dismiss the idea, he takes to the water in a hired boat and, with characteristic indifference, allows himself to drift closer to a dangerous weir. At the point of extreme risk he panics and this occasions an attack of angina.

At first it was just an ache inside his chest, an ache as big as a penny and then it radiated out until it seemed to grip him.

The chest pains which have troubled him throughout the novel have now to be confronted. It is inevitable that Wood should die of a heart attack, of a heart ache that, finding no outward expression, turns in on itself to take a stranglehold on the man. Tom Wood dies in the penultimate chapter at the foot of the stairs in his own house while Henderson and Sarah are in his bed together for the last time.

A bald summary of the plot, however, does less than justice to any novel and this ending may seem to be unacceptably contrived. There is more to the book than that. The character of Tom Wood is well conceived and successfully realised. Though the suggestion of a suppressed

21

attraction for a fellow-officer who died in the war is an important facet of his character, which the novel cannot at this time fully explore, Wood's feelings for Alan Dugdale do offer an explanation for his personal and professional problems after the war. The way in which this is handled in the book would satisfy a future tele-play adaptation, but are too sketchily dealt with to fulfil the expectations of a reader. Having been taken by the novelist so far into the character's soul, one might expect a more central con-sideration of Wood's complex sexual needs.

The characters of Tom and Sarah Wood are, nevertheless, the strength of this novel, and it is in the handling of Andrew Henderson that the main flaws occur. He is the conscripted doctor, at one remove from the discipline of service life and the antics of his colleagues in the mess. Fair and concerned in his professional practice, he is at the same time rebellious and iconoclastic in the face of the officer class and its values. Late in the novel Henderson, on the point of leaving the camp and, soon, the R.A.F., considers his role.

In a sense he and Sarah were allies, like two strangers abandoned outside the city wall. Exiled because they had different gods or because they were poor bell-ringing lepers. Yet it was strange, he mused, that he himself should feel apart from the group, even opposed to them. It had never happened to him before. He had not been particularly con-scious of any intrinsic difference between himself and others. He had only apprehended his otherness since he had been in the R.A.F. And more so over the last month, somehow. Maybe he should be glad of it; as if he had awakened to his own identity, to his own face. So many people wore the wrong faces, they lived lives not their own. And because they wore wrong faces, they lived lives not their own, had children with wrong baby faces, died in wrong beds, even in geographical places they should not have been, if they had followed their own real face to its one, fated destination. He remembered people at school and at University who had not been accepted, who had been bullied, mocked or ignored. The too clever boy, Bert Francis; the very girlish, delicate lad, Graham something or other; a Jewish chap at University with thick lenses in his horn-rimmed glasses that made his bulging eyes owlish and huge; an aggressive and religious Welshman named Dai Ford lobbying Welsh Nationalism with an unnatural hatred; one or two others. The faces swam in the pool of his memory and he fished them up one by one out of the dark—white adolescent faces blinking back at him unhappily. He had never been involved with them very much; he had followed the crowd without being unpleasant to them—but he hadn't accepted them either. Now, though, he felt the minority anger, the minority hurt and pride. The minority sense, though not of being a Welsh Nationalist in England or a Negro amongst white men, or a Jew amongst Christians, but rather the sense of being one and alone amongst the many who cohered together as a crowd. He was the too-clever boy at school, with his worried look and his acne, the aggressive evangelist Welshman, the Jew with thick glasses. He imagined Christ for a moment on the rough improvised cross. Christ, short-sighted and thyrotoxic, staring at the smudged shapes of hostile faces. To understand all is to forgive nothing. Do not forgive them, lest they know what they do, he thought, and then laconically, 'what the hell.'

Just like Wood, Henderson has a depth of feelings from which he shrinks. He feels himself to be different, to be somehow distinguished from his context in as marked a way as those examples that spring into his mind. Yet the strength of feeling which we sense coming from the author himself in that passage is not convincingly enacted in the body of the novel.

Henderson's involvement with the Stewart ménage in the local village is certainly not convincing. Michael, Paul and Marion are never achieved as characters; the bohemianism that they are meant to represent—their disorganised antique shop set in opposition on to the rigidity of the R.A.F. base—is too shallow to offer any escape to Henderson. More importantly, they never persuade the reader that they might engage the central character in that way.

The culmination of Andrew Henderson's decline from respectability, his final break from the world of the officer class, occurs, quite dramatically, at his own 'dining out' meal. His after-dinner speech is a shambles of anger and ineptitude, of incoherence and insult—

I must confess that I haven't been entirely happy; but that is partly my own fault. I am after all a National Serviceman not too willingly conscripted into this way of life not of my own choosing. A doctor—but a National Serviceman nevertheless, who has not been quite at ease, quite at home, despite the many kindnesses so many of you have shown me . . .

At this point somebody said 'Hear, hear' probably out of habit rather than out of any satirical mood.

'. . . However,' Henderson continued, 'one had to face up to realities. I mean the external reality that is visible all around us: the uniforms, the barrage balloons, the homesick faces—and the internal reality: the longing to love someone

*and to be loved, the need for faith in each other and in God,
and the terror of longing for something that one can't quite
understand . . .'*

He could hear somebody coughing the other end of the
dining-room and saw above the table-cloth, above the shining
cutlery and reflections of light on the wine-glasses, a row of
astonished faces, each turned and tilted towards him. He
wasn't sure what he wanted to say. Something perhaps of
his own profound dissatisfaction. He went on though,
involuntarily.

'. . . Not only as a doctor do I know the world is diseased,
not only as a doctor am I aware of a fragment of that same
disease within myself—and in you . . .'

Blenkinsop sitting next to him was pulling on his sleeve,
but Henderson roughly shook him off.

'. . . Indeed the symbols of our sick internal reality,' he
continued, 'are here all about us—are here externalised in the
airship hangars, in the sound of marching feet, in the shocking
uniformity of opinion. We don't know our bogy man—so we
construct him and call him enemy. But what I'm trying to
say is . . .'

In his drunken speech Henderson's feelings are
confused, slurred in the mouth. It is the moment
of his ultimate ostracisation—he is to be cold-
shouldered in the period before his posting and
will slide ignominiously out of the R.A.F.

There is a sense of repulsion at the inherent prejudice in society; one of the concerns central to
Dannie Abse's art is that need to recognise the
tenets of common humanity and ensure that
they are encoded in all our social structures.
Despite Henderson's leaving speech and his
awareness of other outsiders in his life he cannot carry enough weight. The novel fails to

focus and hold those concerns; it is, finally, as unresolved as its central character.

Dannie Abse, at times, the 'outsider' allowed admittance by virtue of his chosen profession, has perhaps been shadow-boxing. Henderson fights as his proxy but has few profound grievances to stoke a real fire in his belly. His 'dining-out' speech draws the expletive 'You dirty Red ——' from Squadron Leader Perry and shortly afterwards it is Perry who leads the other officers in a mess-room games session that turns sourly and violently against Henderson.

Henderson withdraws from the succession of taunts and provocations.

Sober, unwanted, Henderson gladly walked out of the Mess into the decorum of the still night. Through the window he could see them in groups together. He walked away down the cindered path bordered by the neutral fields. Behind him now the Mess was just a dark shape and the lights in the square windows merely sad. He'd just change his uniform and then go for a swim with Marion; purify himself in the waters. He looked up at the sky as he strolled towards Sickquarters.

The problem for the novelist is that he has failed to find an 'objective correlative'. The man who walks away from that ill-treatment is hardly a *Red* and his sensibilities in the midst of the lumberings of a conscript army are not permanently damaged by the experience. Suffering humanity never reaches tragic dimensions here. One is moved more by the railway station scene in ASH ON A YOUNG MAN'S SLEEVE than by anything in this novel.

SOME CORNER OF AN ENGLISH FIELD deserves attention here because it is the only serious novel Dannie Abse has written. After 1956 his feelings find expression through poems, plays and auto-biographical pieces. This novel, though not an unqualified success, has some good writing—Wood's episode on the river especially. One wishes that Dannie Abse had returned to the genre at some point in the three decades of mature writing that have followed.

Dannie Abse published three collections of poems before his next work of fiction. O. JONES, O. JONES. This novel appeared in 1970, fourteen years after SOME CORNER OF AN ENGLISH FIELD. His SELECTED POEMS also appeared in that year. The poems are of much more significance. However, O. JONES, O. JONES represents Dannie Abse's most obvious attempt to reach a mass audience for the book is clearly within that sub-genre of British book and screenplay writing—the medical school picaresque.

In common with most other doctors, his experience of medical school, in Cardiff and later in London, encompassed the energetic, impressionable, and at times wayward years of his early and mid-twenties. He draws on material from those years in A POET IN THE FAMILY, and in some of his poetry from the 1960s his experience as a qualified doctor begins to shape poems—notably 'Pathology of colours' and 'The smile was'. However, O. JONES, O. JONES, dedicated *To Vernon Scannell who suggested that I should write this book . . .*, fails to organise those earlier experiences into a fiction that has the lasting significance of the poems.

Ozymandias (formerly Herbert) Jones is the Abse figure—his body in London and his heart in Cardiff—and the novel is narrated by him. Perhaps that is a major error, because too often the perspective is strained and the humour forced. Moments of serious thought are almost intrusive—as when, in 1968, Ozy and his friend Basil witness the peace march on the American Embassy in Grosvenor Square—

Already the sun was going down behind the buildings, a dazzle of silver and orange on the highest office windows, and still the procession filed past the Square, group after group with their identity placards: THE CAMBRIDGE LABOUR PARTY, THE UNION OF LIBERAL STUDENTS, THE IRISH WORKERS' GROUP, and always they waved slogans like STOP YANKEE BUTCHERS NOW and VIETNAM FOR THE VIETNAMESE.

'It's bloody awful, isn't it?' I said to Basil.

'What is?'

'The world.'

I meant the way it was organized. The way they slew people, the mathematics of death. 'Wars and all that,' I said inarticulately to Basil. Somehow that touched Basil off. He embarked on a long speech that shook me. About how being a doctor was a divine privilege, how one could be of so much use, committed to no dogma but to humankind, by doing one's job with dedication and selflessness; how each one of us could make marginally the world less bloody, less miserable, less contaminated. And though this speech of his was decorated with old clichés, Basil addressed me so sincerely and with such passion that I felt uplifted. I suddenly felt I had to be a doctor. I suddenly knew that I too wanted to be useful, to be of service to someone else—perhaps in a sour, curtained room —to say, 'Yes, I will.'

That same incident informs the poem 'Demo Against the Vietnam War, 1968'. Challenged (by a cynical visitor) to celebrate just one thing about London Dannie Abse chooses

> *. . . that tatty group, under Nelson's column,*
> *Their home-made banners held aloft,*

It is another example of the way in which Abse feels able to use the same material to serve different functions in his writing. In the novel the Grosvenor Square march crystallizes the element of seriousness and idealism which Jones feels inside him. An onlooker, he is made to relate that display of commitment to his own circumstances. Dannie Abse, in his own poem, the writer in early middle-age rather than the young medical student, places the idealism in a harsher, more cynical context.

So praise to the end of the march, their songs, their jargon, outside the Embassy. Yes, this I'd choose: their ardour, their naiveté, violence of commitment, cruelty of devotion, 'We shall not be moved, We shall overcome'—despite sullen police concealed in vans waiting for arclights to fail, for furtive darkness and camera-teams, dismantled, all breezing home.

Basically on the side of the demonstrators, he nonetheless proceeds by a series of questioning epithets: their 'violence of commitment' is matched by the 'sullen police' in their 'furtive darkness'; their 'cruelty of devotion' has been mediated by a camera team 'dismantled' at the end of the event, 'breezing home' dispassionately.

In the novel, that incident marks the beginning of a more serious determination on the part of Ozymandias Jones to apply himself. The trouble is that Jones, unlike Abse, is not a sufficiently notable figure to make one care. It is, however, interesting to note at another point the way in which Dannie Abse has drawn on the facts of his own life which underpinned ASH ON A YOUNG MAN'S SLEEVE. At the end of that book the author was left deep in thought before a waterfall in the park. His second book has Ozy Jones in the bohemian Cairo Café thinking of his boyhood in Cardiff. This time the waterfall is desecrated.

For my part I began to think of home, of our house in Sandringham Road, Cardiff. My room there overlooked a bit of a park called Waterloo Gardens. A washed-clean stream threaded its way through patches of different greens and, at one point, its slow waters accelerated into a crashing waterfall. Sometimes, when I was a schoolboy, after encountering small disappointments, I used to sit beside that waterfall. I used to stare at it, listen to it, until I became lost from myself and consoled therefore. Once, when I was about fourteen, one moonless winter night, I climbed the railings of that closed, dark and abandoned park. I brushed through bosky paths until I stood on the banks of the stream which, in the dark, I could hear but could not see. I pissed into it, all the while looking up at the spreading stars.

The quality of that experience is deliberately undercut, as befits an anti-hero. Unfortunately, Ozy Jones is no Jimmy Porter, nor is he Dylan's

'Young Dog.' Perhaps the book fails because none of the characters or the incidents goes far enough. The consultant, Titmus, is never as blustering and irascible as James Robertson Justice; the student antics are too few and too safe. What might have worked as a lively picaresque, never finds the focus, the plot, the drive to carry a reader along in the way that Tom Sharpe or Leslie Thomas might.

It is notable that towards the end of the book a short scene occurs with Jones again sitting at his regular table in the Cairo Café. He is engaged in conversation by the proud parents of Vernon, a successful advertising copy-writer, making his way in London. This isolated incident, explored over four pages, contributes nothing to the plot or the characterisation of Ozy Jones, except that he is given the opportunity to tell them a story about Mr Haines *our leading brain surgeon at the hospital*, probing desperately for a tumour in his patient's brain. The man, in those days under a local anaesthetic, protested aloud in a startling way:

'It seems the surgeon could not find the tumour,' I continued, 'and he kept on pushing his probe this way and that way, trying to feel out for the resistant tumour tissue. Of course, all the time he did this he had to destroy normal brain cells.'
'The patient was awake?' asked Vernon's father, startled.
'Yes,' I said. 'Anyway, again and again the surgeon explored the brain unsuccessfully with his probe. The operating theatre was utterly silent until the surgeon was interrupted in his explorations by an unearthly voice which said, "Stop interfering with my soul, stop interfering with my

soul, stop interfering with my soul." The patient could not stop repeating that phrase over and over.

The visiting couple find this story embarrassingly serious, and leave. That same story was, in fact, related to Dannie Abse by his brother Wilfred who was assisting the eminent Lambert Rogers at that very operation. It leads to one of Abse's finest performance poems 'In the theatre', first published with 'Demo against the Vietnam War, 1968' in his fourth collection FUNLAND AND OTHER POEMS two years after O. JONES, O. JONES appeared.

> *'Leave my soul alone, leave my soul alone,'*
> *that voice so arctic and that cry so odd*
> *had nowhere else to go—till the antique*
> *gramophone wound down and the words began*
> *to blur and slow, '. . . leave . . . my soul*
> *. . . alone . . .'*
> *to cease at last when something other died.*
> *And silence matched the silence under snow.*

The poem, especially that ending, invariably chills any audience at a reading. It is a fine example of the way that Dannie Abse can create a tautly-structured narrative with his sense of subtle rhyme and rhythm; The insistent 'go . . . slow . . . snow' winding the voice down to a shivering silence.

Certain stories haunt Dannie Abse and recur in his work. The best of that work is frequently rooted in autobiography. O. JONES, O. JONES fails because the material from the writer's time at medical school is, over fifteen years later, intractable—at least in that comic novel's form.

It seems that this writer works most assuredly when he writes honestly within the spirit of his own life. That fact seems to be acknowledged after O. JONES, O. JONES for his next book of prose, published four years later, was a full-scale autobiography—A POET IN THE FAMILY.

A POET IN THE FAMILY is in three parts, two of which concentrate on the writer's experience of college days in London, from January 1943 to the spring of 1965, shortly after his father's death. However, the opening third of the book covers, in nine brief chapters, some of the formative aspects of Dannie Abse's early life in Cardiff. This has to provide a background to the poet's work, but it also has to offer a resumé and an expansion for the reader who has previously read ASH ON A YOUNG MAN'S SLEEVE.

On the whole, this first part of the book works well enough. There are, inevitably, repetitions, but the interest derived from receiving familiar material in a quite different way is probably sufficient compensation. For example, the Jimmy Ford of ASH ON A YOUNG MAN'S SLEEVE is here named as Sid Hamm. The important character of Keith Thomas in the earlier book does not appear and it is Mr. Davies, the Abses' neighbour and local A.R.P. warden, who is killed in an air-raid.

In its second part the reader follows Dannie Abse's progress from his arrival in London to his qualification as a doctor at Westminster Hospital in London. The general circumstances of O. JONES, O. JONES and several specific scenes from that novel re-appear in this section, though the action is now placed in the actual years of the war. The Swiss Cottage flat from which Ozy is evicted is clearly 38, Aberdare Gardens, and Mrs Frankel and Mrs Mayer appear as themselves— Mrs Schiff and Mrs Blumenfeld. In fact the author at times simply lifts whole paragraphs from the 1970 novel to include in this auto-biography.

This is a characteristic of the body of Dannie Abse's work: an incident, character or a scene may prove so striking, so significant for him that it serves as the occasion for a poem, the core of a story or a scene in a play. Dannie Abse obviously subscribes to William Carlos Williams' view that *Nine Tenths of our lives is well forgotten in the living*. From what remains the writer has to fashion all his work.

The first section of A POET IN THE FAMILY had been prefaced by a quotation from the American poet Williams advising that autobiography should be refined until,

A thin thread of narrative remains—a few hundred pages about which clusters, like rock candy, the interests upon which the general reader will spend a few hours, as might a sweet-toothed child, preferring something richer and not so hard on the teeth.

(The Autobiography)

Abse's task is to retell the accessible events of his life. While holding to the facts. He must organise his narrative so that its pace and interest will engage the reader. We expect movement and a succession of cameo characters.

The middle section of the book traces the way in which Dannie Abse comes to terms with the two major aspects of his life, as a doctor and as a writer—'*Riding two horses*' he calls it.

The former profession, particularly in those years of training, seems to have caused more serious problems than his writing. As a medical student Dannie Abse experiences the embarrassments, faux-pas and self-doubts perhaps inevitable to the nature of that calling. However, as a writer he enjoyed early success during that time. In June 1946 his first book of poems AFTER EVERY GREEN THING was accepted by Hutchinson, though the book did not appear until February 1949. They have remained the major publishers of his poetry and prose ever since.

Dannie Abse is now dismissive of that early work:

I see now that that first book of mine contained for the most part linguistically florid and faulty poems.

The book is not listed in his COLLECTED POEMS 1948–1976 and the poet himself always talks apologetically about it. It is important, though, to note that the collection left Dannie Abse with a deeper realisation of the issues which his two callings now raised:

The general public tend to think of poets, when they think of them at all, as 'sensitive plants', as peculiar, vulnerable personages who have been born with one skin less than other mortals and who, therefore, congenitally deficient in ordinary armour, feel too much.

Thus Rainer Maria Rilke admitted he did not like leaving a bar of soap behind in an hotel bedroom in case it felt lonely! Most poets are not that dotty, but to be able to identify oneself closely with another human being, to become the music while the music lasts, on occasions may be an advantage. It is not an advantage, for the most part, in the practice of medicine. Doctors, possibly, may make good poets; but poets rarely make good doctors. The good doctor's ability to distance himself from his patient's suffering is helpful, finally, for the patient.

He came to the realisation that the artist must address himself to large themes, though he will, of necessity, work from the firm basis of his own experiences.

The poems in AFTER EVERY GREEN THING *hardly touched at all on public themes. They were too private.*

It is that new-found 'distance' that led Dannie Abse to respond to a commission for an article on contemporary Hebrew poetry by inventing a poet called Dov Shamir and 'translating' the 'Song for Dov Shamir'. Sending a batch of poems to be received by T. S. Eliot some months later he found that particular poem to be received most enthusiastically. It appeared subsequently in his 1952 collection WALKING UNDER WATER. The incident underlines the humour and playfulness with language and situations that characterise this writer. Abse writes because he has a need to write; but it is often a very enjoyable business.

In the 1950s a deeper, less indulgent poetry was emerging from Dannie Abse's experiences. Poems were being sought at the heart of *the forensic prose of the occasion*, and though it was to be a number of years before the poet's medical life would directly inform the poems, that determination to involve poetry centrally in his life and to answer the challenges of living directly through his poetry was to be put to the test in sad circumstances.

The remaining third of A POET IN THE FAMILY covers the early years of Dannie Abse's marriage (in 1951) to Joan Mercer, their three children— Keren, Susanna and David—and briefly, his period of National Service in the R.A.F. which formed the basis of his second novel, SOME CORNER OF AN ENGLISH FIELD. He wrote ASH ON A YOUNG MAN'S SLEEVE whilst working at the R.A.F. chest clinic in London and then in the 1960s became regularly involved in public poetry readings. In this he was encouraged by Jeremy Robson who would later publish POETRY DIMENSION annually with Abse as its editor. Robson also, in 1983, brought out Joseph Cohen's THE POETRY OF DANNIE ABSE, a collection of critical essays on the poet's work.

His early years in London saw Dannie Abse founding his own poetry magazine, POETRY AND POVERTY. He also figured prominently in that strange literary skirmish involving 'The Movement' and 'The Mavericks'—that odd affair into which many of the leading poets of the post-war years found themselves drawn. But I shall look more closely at the significance of that when I come to discuss Abse's poetry in more detail.

37

However, while literary and professional links were being forged in this period, the most telling event of those years was the death of Dannie Abse's father.

In the summer of 1964 the poet returned from his first American reading tour to find that his father's health had deteriorated. *He had become a pulmonary cripple.* He was admitted to Llandough Hospital, a few miles from Cardiff and, two months later, he died. Dannie Abse and his brother Wilfred, doctors both, were powerless onlookers.

In the solarium I climbed on to a bed, lay back and gazed upwards through the glass roof at the clear night sky with all its humbling lights until I experienced some brief, small refreshment. While my brother catnapped on the next bed it seemed to me that a huge inhuman right hand held up the spinning earth while the left hand reached up higher and higher to light the furthest stars. Nearer, conspicuous, the moon hung mercilessly white. I did not know then, that never again would I be able to see a moon anywhere in the world, moon distinct and round, or moon a mere sliver, or a swollen mist-crashing moon appearing low on the horizon, without remembering my father, my father dying.

Later that morning, my father irrevocably dead, Wilfred said to me, 'No man who has ever watched his father die can ever be quite the same man again.'

I became mortal the night my father died.

The trauma of that experience marks out the strongest poems in his next collection, A SMALL DESPERATION, published in 1968. These poems are 'In Llandough Hospital', 'Two Small Stones' and 'Interview with a Spirit Healer'. In his following collection, FUNLAND AND OTHER POEMS, 1973, the fine 'Peachstone' owes its genesis to the moment when his father, in hospital, sucks the peach that Huldah, Dannie's sister, has brought him.

From this point the poet and the doctor will be

. . . increasingly aware, too, of his own mortality—how the apple flesh was always turning brown after the bite.

His life is shaped by these two callings: at times they are the two horses he rides. He strives to make the poetry horse Pegasus rather than a wooden rocker. At times he feels himself, as Chekhov had, to be hunting 'after two hares'—

I turned to scrutinise the X-rays on the blazing screens again and thought of how Chekhov had once written in a letter, 'You advise me not to hunt after two hares . . . I feel more confident and more satisfied with myself when I reflect that I have two professions and not one. Medicine is my lawful wife and literature is my mistress. When I get tired of one I spend the night with the other; though it's disorderly, it's not dull, and besides, neither of them loses anything from my infidelity.'

Almost a decade after writing this autobiography, Dannie Abse, in a lecture entitled 'Pegasus and the Rocking Horse', developed these discussions of the role of the artist. He reacts to what he sees as an archaic, romantic view of the artist's role:

How romantically one such as Jung discusses the Poet with a capital P. 'Art', he writes in MODERN MAN IN SEARCH OF A SOUL, 'is a kind of innate drive that seizes a human being and makes him its instrument. The artist is not a person endowed with free will who seeks his own ends but one who allows art to realize its purposes through him . . . To perform this difficult office it is sometimes necessary for him to sacrifice happiness and everything that makes life worth living for the ordinary human being.'

The impression one has of Dannie Abse, from both the man and his work, is much more level-headed. Because his writing is, in the main, worked from his own experiences, he has created a body of work that is accessible and engaging. The circumstances of his life have some remarkable aspects, but out of that life he has celebrated, and continues to celebrate

. . . everything that makes life worth living for the ordinary human being.

One accepts the situations of his poetry and prose because Dannie Abse, early in his career, worked to develop a voice that has a natural, convincing timbre. As he says in 'A Voice of My Own'—

I think it no accident that as the years pass by I use more and more a conversational tone rather than a singing one.

That concern with 'voice', with the 'conversational tone' is brought to bear at length in Dannie Abse's writing for the theatre. In the 1960s and 1970s a substantial proportion of the writer's energy was directed into play-writing. Mindful of the notable, and in some cases disastrous forays into Theatre by accomplished poets, he was wary of launching himself into that quite distinct medium. But his continuing commitment to the Theatre has some real achievement to record. It also contributes much to one's understanding of the poetry that forms the central and primary medium for Dannie Abse.

Between the publication of SOME CORNER OF AN ENGLISH FIELD and POEMS, GOLDERS GREEN Dannie Abse's first play was performed. In 1960 HOUSE OF COWARDS, commissioned by the Questors Theatre in London, received its first performance from that company. Some thirteen years earlier he had approached the theatre's director, Alfred Emmett, with a verse play, FIRE IN HEAVEN. It proved unsuitable, but when the theatre launched its annual Festival of New Plays, Dannie Abse was approached again and the three-act HOUSE OF COWARDS was readily accepted. It was a success, winning the Charles Henry Foyle New Play Award, and confirming a valuable, creative relationship between the poet and that theatre.

In 1962 the Questors Festival staged the one-act GONE, and in 1964 a two-act play IN THE CAGE which re-worked and extended the theme from Balzac's story 'The Executioner' which in turn had previously inspired Dannie Abse's first attempt at play-writing—FIRE IN HEAVEN.

HOUSE OF COWARDS explored a theme which Dannie Abse had first dealt with in his poem 'The Meeting'. This piece, included in his collection TENANTS OF THE HOUSE (1957), seems stretched between Samuel Beckett's WAITING FOR GODOT and T. S. Eliot's PRUFROCK & OTHER POEMS.

41

Where has the Speaker been all these years? Rinse your eyes from gardens, follow the railway lines. Come nearer to the dream in the halls of mean cities. Enter, imagine, listen: the cry down the flight of stairs, the squeak of chairs, a floor without carpets; as of old, on Babel, murmur of many languages. But one dream.

Stroll then to the eternal meeting through streets tangled like string, walk over square shadows of shops, dark shops that sell only a synthetic dream, cross under the hoardings of advertisements. Melancholy spring, springtime, dust, petrol, blossoms of carbon monoxide. Here, here, in the backstreets of any city, the one dream.

The play chooses to focus on a set of characters in one house in one of the 'mean cities'. The sham-cripple Hicks and his compliant wife; their listless son, George; the lodger and latent paedophile, Alf, from Wales; the bogus widow Miss Chantry—all these people have cause to wait on the arrival of 'the Speaker.'

At its opening, and at intervals throughout, loudspeaker-vans proclaim his impending appearance at The Sunshine Hall. The Speaker, of course does not arrive and the newshound from THE DAILY STAR (an inspired projection by Abse) who has promised to feature the Hicks family and the Speaker's stay at their house, moves on to riper prospects of a story.

HICKS: *You . . . and the Daily Star. You're muck, that's what you are. And your paper.*

JAY: *The paper? Why, there's no need to abuse 'The Daily Star.' It just reflects you, that's all. What you want: the glamour that you have not but would like, the violence you would indulge in, but dare*

42

not. It's your dreams in black and white, and if they seem cheap and sensational and sentimental, that's what they are.

GEORGE: *That's not true. It leaves out too much. It's slanted.*

JAY: *Sometimes they go wrong. That's natural. I'm just employed by them and not responsible for everything. Anyway I believe in what I write.*

HICKS: *You're vile.*

JAY: *I wanted to be a serious writer once. When I was twenty. But that's a lot of crap when you have responsibilities as I have. The editor said, get a story of the Speaker, a personal story—nothing abstract. That's what I've tried to do. You'll read my piece and it'll be a good workmanlike job. That's something, you know. I'm not ashamed of that.*

HICKS: *You used us.*

JAY: *You wanted to be used. You only had to say 'No' right at the beginning.*

What he leaves behind is truly a 'house of cowards', but although each character's lack of willpower or vision has been implied in the body of the play, the confirmation of their hypocrisy comes about in a crude dénouement of mutual accusations or spontaneous confessions.

It is the non-appearance of the Speaker which occasions the trauma for each of them, but the effect is less than convincing. This Messiah, whether spiritual or political, never inspires the action in his absence, as Beckett's Godot does. Perhaps it is that 1, Shelley Street lacks the dramatic urgency of Beckett's stark and tortured setting. I think that the real flaw lies in the play's lack of focus: we don't care enough about these people—their social condition or the state of their souls. The language is never as taut as Beckett's or the characters as complex as Osborne's Jimmy Porter in Look Back in Anger, performed four years earlier, though one senses that both plays inform Dannie Abse's approach and commitment to the Theatre.

Only the character of Mr Nott has real interest. Nott is closer to Pinter's 'Caretaker' Aston than Alf Jenkins is to his 'Welsh' tramp Davies. Like Aston, Nott has emerged from a mental institution less than the person he was, but a more significant character, showing the stigmata of his mind.

Sheila: *Then you're from a mental hospital?*
Nott: *I was, yes.*
Sheila: *You escaped?*
Nott: *No, no, no. I've been discharged. They purged me of every bizarre dream. My name is Nott. Nott like my father and his father before him. You're still puzzled. Of course, I haven't explained. I used to think I was Mr. Morley or Mr. Neely or Mr. Dixon. Ordinary people. Nothing special. I just wanted to be anybody but myself—that's how they explained it to me. Wanting to be someone else is half the trouble; when you believe yourself to be another person, however commonplace, that puts the lid on it. Psychotic delusions, yes. Still with insulin shocks, I became myself again. Plain Mr. Nott.*

The intervention of medicine into the psyche and soul of a patient is a fascination that Dannie Abse most memorably records in his poem 'In

the Theatre' and most fully develops in his 1976
play PYTHAGORAS. Our interest in Nott, though,
is never pursued as the play expands on ideas
about freedom and media manipulation contained in 'The Meeting'.

Night. Moonshine on rooftops, pegs on empty washing lines,
barking of dogs, blue television light behind curtains,
whimper of a distant locomotive like a child's impotent cry.
Discontent of voices. One dream.

The eternal meeting and exit exit exit exit.
Still the audience waits for the Speaker,
here, everywhere, forever—waits in the dim hall,
watching an x-rayed hand scrawling on the wall,
waits, waits, with a yawn, a crossing of legs, and a cough.

In HOUSE OF COWARDS however, the original
conception embodied in the poem is stretched
to breaking point. Imagery that proved a little
too derivative in the early poem is projected
dramatically through less than convincing
characters woven into a heavy, predictable plot.

Two years later the one-act GONE was produced
at The Questors Theatre Festival. Set in a London
studio-apartment, this piece has two actors playing the roles of rivals for the love of Connie, who
has left her older husband Peter. The studio has
a set of bar-bells—Peter is thirteen years older
than his wife and needs to work out in order to
'compete'. His visitor, Aubrey, has come in search
of Connie and makes little attempt to disguise
his desire for her. They argue about the bar-bells,
about the healthiness of various foods—at one
point struggling over a jam sandwich—and vie

with each other over their respective relationships with Connie.

This short play aims to create the sort of suppressed tension and violence that Harold Pinter was establishing as his characteristic style at this time. The dislocation of characters from everyday social context; their use of language as both a defensive and offensive weapon; the significance accruing to domestic objects; the exchange of banal information—these are all vital ingredients of the early Pinter plays.

As the curtain falls in GONE and Aubrey leaves Peter apparently preparing to hang himself from the rope that has been threateningly suspended from a rafter throughout the play, we hear the calls of a rag and bone man out in the street. Could this be a conscious echo of Yeats' 'The Circus Animals' Desertion'?

> *I must lie down where all the ladders start,*
> *In the foul rag-and-bone shop of the heart.*

The play just cannot bear that weight, or aspire to that significance. It remains a self-conscious piece.

What is interesting is that fifteen years later Dannie Abse should go back to this short piece and re-work it into a full-length play.

In 1977 GONE became GONE IN JANUARY. It was staged at the Edinburgh Festival and again at the Young Vic the following year. The single act is developed into a second act in which Connie appears with her new lover, Tony Pickerall. Peter's threatened hanging is defused as both he and Aubrey measure themselves against Pickerall. The sexual innuendoes and jibes exchanged between the two of them are undercut and made ridiculous by Connie's clear assumption of Tony Pickerall as her current lover. He is a professional musician whose jazz trio has just completed an engagement in Eastbourne. Connie has been with him and flaunts the encounter. She has made up her mind to move out and live permanently with Tony in Paddington.

In addition to the sexual rivalries there is added another complication—Tony Pickerall is a West Indian. The underlying tensions come together in one cryptic exchange between Connie and Peter in the last few minutes of the play. Connie is talking about her day back in school:

CONNIE: *Most of the kids had one brother or one sister but one child—aged twelve but reading age of five, if that—had fourteen brothers and sisters, he really did. He counted them on his fingers, said all their names. He was embarrassed by it because he couldn't get all the names on the form.* (voice trails off) *West Indian boy.*

PETER: *You don't even like jazz. I've got no racial prejudice you know Connie—haven't I studied African politics, African Medicine, read the anthropological literature? But this is different. Connie don't be foolish. Why make life so difficult for yourself? This is white man's land.*
(Connie flinches)

CONNIE: *That time I came back from the hospital you said I'd feel different after a holiday.*

47

PETER: *I remember. We went to Cornwall, Christ, not Eastbourne, five years ago. Great holiday, blue day after blue day, sky and sea.*

CONNIE: *All I heard were the seagulls crying—all the time—like babies.*

PETER: *You never told me.*

CONNIE: *I've never told you how often I dream I'm touching the fontanelle of a baby's head. I'm out of touch with something elemental and eternal. Do you understand?*

PETER: *Henry Rule, Aubrey, this Pickerall idiot, these are all* in *touch I suppose?*

CONNIE: *I wasn't talking about them.*
        (Pause)

This effectively clarifies and deepens the odd relationships which the play has unfolded. It ends with Connie making a wish over the expensive birthday cake which Peter has bought for her. He blows out the candles. She leaves and then he methodically bursts all the party balloons with his cigarette.

This ending is effective theatre and compensates to a degree for weaknesses that the play inherits from its original version. The relationship between Peter and Aubrey is still less than convincing though, and their conversations continue to lean towards the Pinteresque, whilst never quite creating the effect of a chilling threat to each member of the audience, that characterises Pinter's best work.

The third Questor play is IN THE CAGE. Based on an incident in Balzac's short story 'The Executioner', it is set in an unspecified country, in the present. A military regime rules the land and subjugates its people. The play focuses on a family which is implicated in an act of terrorism which in fact has been perpetrated by one of the two sons, David. His brother Chris is a pacifist but it is Chris who is chosen to fulfil the authorities' reprisal on the community by executing the other members of his family.

Two areas of dramatic interplay are created: the family argues its moral and political position as the threat of reprisal hangs over it; at the same time the army captain faces his own sense of duty. He must resolve the dilemma into which he has been put by his general's order: can he, should he conduct the plan for reprisals?

Chris executed his father but has been unable to continue down the line. He is mad at the end of the play and tells the story of a childhood experience when his father ordered him to commit an act of cruelty. On a winter morning his horse would not take a steep slippery hill road. His father says that next time he should place straw under the animal and light it.

CHRIS: *The mist like milk, the sun breaking through the mist and me a fool of a boy lighting the straw. It was primitive, wasn't it? But I had, you see, no qualms then. My father told me to. Don't blame me. His was the voice of authority so I had no choice. You can't expect a child to feel responsible. That's the truth. Go ask, my father he'll bear me out.*

The play ends with light fading on the impassive general at his desk.

Dannie Abse is concerned to examine the nature of responsibility in public actions and personal morality: one senses the weight of Nazi war crimes behind this play. What is the nature of authority in a strictly depersonalised system? In his poems and plays Abse constantly affirms the power of conscience, and the moral responsibility that occasions guilt.

Six years after this play was performed the poet visits Germany and finds:

> *The German streets tonight*
> *are soaped in moonlight*
> *The streets of Germany are clean*
> *like the hands of Lady Macbeth*
> (No More Mozart)

The sense of guilt is necessary, it is a moral imperative. One does not wash it away.

That poem from 1970 can be seen as a link between IN THE CAGE and the more fully realised play THE DOGS OF PAVLOV (1972) which dramatises Professor Milgram's Yale experiments into authority and obedience. As the Corporal says to one of his men IN THE CAGE:

CORPORAL: *You're soft hearted, very soft hearted, you are. Aw, this sort of thing 'appens all the time. It's not just us. Remember Hungary, Cyprus, Algeria, Congo, and all them other places you read about in the papers? It went on yesterday there, it'll continue in some other place tomorrow. It's timeless, that's a foaming fact.*

50

However, the major weaknesses of IN THE CAGE resulted from its determination to make a universal point through unspecified location and vaguely representative characters. The talking heads are recognisably 'English', but don't engage our emotional involvement. Dannie Abse's next work for the theatre proved much stronger because it drew on the energy of a specific event —the controversy resulting from the Yale University experiments. The characters, though not totally convincing, are now located and the dramatic realisation of the piece draws on the strength of the documented context of Milgram's work.

This takes the form of a laboratory in which volunteers are ordered to address mathematical questions to subjects strapped to a seat behind glass. Wrong answers are to be punished by administering electric shocks of increasing intensity. The questioners are told that this is valuable scientific work, all in the pursuit of a learning process analysis. In fact, the suffering answerer is an actress, Sally Parsons, employed by Yale University. It is the questioners who are really the subjects of the experiment and Milgram's concern is to assess the power of an authoritarian structure to suspend the natural force of our human sympathy. Sally writhes and screams realistically as her punishment intensifies. None of the questioners relinquishes the punishment lever. None did in the actual Yale experiment.

Dannie Abse's play develops the personality of the actress–victim and its climax has Sally's fiancé Kurt tricked by her into volunteering for the experiment. Kurt, who is, rather unecessarily I think, half-German, realises the nature of the compromise and denounces the experiment and its originators. They are, he says, in a morally indefensible position. Their deception has profound implications for they have only the shallow self-interested excuse that

. . . it's for the fatherland. The fatherland of Science

This, coming from Kurt, is a weighty, key statement. We must not only criticise the recent past in Germany, but also recognise what we all have in common with that fascist movement. I feel that Kurt is used in this play in almost as pointed a way as the German au-pair girl in the earlier poem 'A Night Out' from A SMALL DESPERATION. Germans and Germany are emotionally charged subjects in Dannie Abse's writing, as I shall make clear in my consideration of the poems.

When THE DOGS OF PAVLOV was published it was prefaced by a letter from Professor Stanley Milgram acknowledging the complexity of the issues his experiments had raised and entering a dialogue with the writer. A student who took part in the second series of Milgram's experiments was so moved by the self-awareness he experienced that he succeeded in claiming conscientious objector status when called up in the Vietnam draft of 1970. Milgram pleads:

As a dramatist you surely understand that illusion may serve a revelatory function, and indeed, the very possibility of theatre is founded on the benign use of contrivance.

52

Dannie Abse clearly is aware of those possibilities in this play. Handling profound and current issues, THE DOGS OF PAVLOV was his strongest play to date. Its intellectual and moral concern was matched by an effective theatrical conception that proved particularly striking in the laboratory scenes and in Sally's dream sequence. In this her mind projects a strangely contorted ballet of figures who chant racial and sexist slogans. The whole is counterpointed by flatly stated statistics.

GORDON: *Your favourite flower?*
KURT: *Carnations?*
GORDON: *No*
KURT: *Roses*
GORDON: *No*
KURT: *Black roses?*
GORDON: *No. Daisies! Daisies! Daisies!*
KURT: *Black daisies. I love her black daisies.*
GORDON: *Good boy, now you've got it. The twist of vision. Now you're talking. Now you can see in the dark. Good boy.*
(Gordon signals to the 'chorus')
ALL: (satirically) *Go-od boy.*
KURT: (joyful) *Luminous black daisies. Huge funeral rain-washed, black daisies.*
(Gordon slowly claps. Kurt and then 'chorus' join him in clapping. Kurt rushes to a raised level on the stage.)
Where are they working—in the Midlands, in Yorkshire—there they are in the mill, in the factory, in the foundry, in the brick kiln.
HARLEY: *They are taking our jobs from us.*
KURT: *All those unpleasant, unskilled jobs.*
ALL: *Hear, hear.*

53

KURT: *The night shifts in the mills, for example, are*
          carried out exclusively by black immigrants.
ALL: *Sieg heil, sieg heil, sieg heil.*

Dannie Abse is determined that his audience shall
be aware of the implications of the Yale experiment. Obedience may well be a product not of
idealism and duty, but rather of prejudice,
ignorance and fear.

The Yale laboratory enabled Dannie Abse to
create a bizarre context of moral and emotional
aberrations, but at about the same time he had
written a long poem in nine sections called
'Funland' in which the world was seen to be a
sort of mental asylum in its entirety. In 1971 the
piece was broadcast on Radio 3 and the text was
later taken up by students at the New College of
Speech and Drama who dramatised the poem for
performance. Dannie Abse was prompted by this
to develop his original idea and so a further
dramatisation was presented at The Questors
Festival of 1975. Gary O'Connor's review of that
performance in THE FINANCIAL TIMES, pointed
out that the character of Pythagoras might well
prove to be the real focus of the drama. And that
is what happened. The following year PYTHAGORAS
was performed at the Birmingham Repertory
Theatre. It has proved the most successful of
Dannie Abse's works for the theatre, receiving
good notices and continuing to be performed in
the repertory of amateur groups.

Much that is central to the writer comes together
in the conception and imagery of this play, and
Abse himself regards the piece as his only truly

successful drama. In an HTV interview with
Emyr Daniel in 1983 the poet is asked whether
his brother Leo is fair in his remark that Dannie
should stick to poetry. His reply suggests that
perhaps Leo has not seen PYTHAGORAS. He
continues:

*Well, I've written one very good play. I'm very proud of it—
it's called* PYTHAGORAS. *It's about a magician called
Pythagoras Smith, who, incidentally, once performed at
Porthcawl Pavilion. I think that's a pretty good play.*

It is. The original poem 'Funland' raised issues
and created possibilities that its form could not
fully explore. It is a strange piece, not without its
own energy and wit: many of the ingredients of
the stage play are indeed evident in the poem:

> *With considerable poise*
> *the superintendent*
> *has been sitting for hours now*
> *at the polished table*
>
> *Outside the tall window*
> *all manner of items*
> *have been thundering down*
> *boom boom stagily*
> *the junk of heaven*

Fat Blondie, Marian, and of course Pythagoras
himself, all have their genesis in the poem,
though the abiding presence of the world therein
is the narrator's 'atheist uncle.'

The poem's motley procession of characters and
references, its lack of a clear, linear narrative,

create a surreal effect that is confusing and disturbing. One is made to work for associations between the sections and to respond to unrelated characters and disparate allusions. The result is an existentialist work which reflects elements of the Theatre of the Absurd. At its centre is the absence of an ultimate purpose. When the stone is rolled aside no one emerges, not even Godot.

> *They are all dead replied uncle*
> *don't you know yet*
>   *all of them dead –*
> *gone where they don't play billiards*
> *haven't you heard the news?*
>
> *And Elijah the meths drinker*
> *what about Elijah I asked*
> *who used to lie on a parkbench*
> *in bearded sleep—he too?*
>
> *Of course sneered uncle*
> *smashed smashed years ago like the rest of them*
> *gone with the ravens gone with the lightning*
> *Why else each springtime*
> *with the opening of a door*
> *no-one's there?*
>
> *Now at the midnight ritual*
> *we invoked Elijah Merlin Mesmer the best of them*
> *gone with the ravens gone with the lightning*
> *as we stand as usual in concentric circles*
> *around the thornbush*
> *Something will happen tonight.*

When this material is developed for the theatre it becomes more readily accessible. However, in the transition that disturbingly surreal power of the poem is diffused. The paradox of the narrator's imagination sparkling and crackling within the confines of an asylum becomes effectively theatrical as Pythagoras Smith draws on his magical powers in the Superintendent's Office or in the grounds of the hospital. Theatricality demands that the man's magical madness is externalised and we are more comfortable viewing such things as members of an audience. The very effectiveness of Pythagoras Smith's magical tricks involves us in the experience of theatre. As he controls thunder and lightning, as he burns or freezes with his magical wand, we are seduced by the possibility of his supernatural powers. From the first scene we comply with the reactions—pain and fear—of the Nurse and Charlie, and we have a vested interest in our eponymous hero's uniqueness.

Pythagoras may be an asylum inpatient, but, surrounded by 'white coats', he alone wears the 'purple cloak':

PYTHAGORAS: *Difficult to wear both the white coat of*
science and the magician's purple one. You
have to be . . . very great. (pause)
White coat and purple coat
a sleeve from both he sews.
That white is always stained with blood
that purple by the rose.
BIDDY: *Very good. Arthur'd like that.*
PYTHAGORAS: *And phantom rose and blood most real*
compose a hybrid style,
white coat and purple coat
few men can reconcile.

This man is composed of the two main elements of his creator—he assumes the role of the doctor at several points in the play; he wants to control events, he wants to rule over the other patients and staff: at other times he is imagination pushed to and beyond the limits of sanity. He rhymes like a poet; he has vision beyond his immediate surroundings and, within the theatrical world of the play (and also within the theatrical play at the asylum), he is able to 'reconcile' both elements of his and our nature. Pythagoras is, at brief moments, both in the world and escaping it.

The poem 'Funland' ends with

> *Do not wake us. We may die.*

That is an intriguing paradox. It implies that we may, in fact, be fully alive only at such times as we inhabit the state of our imagination. It has echoes of T. S. Eliot's Prufrock who sees fantasy and desire indulged

> *Till human voices wake us and we drown*

Abse acknowledges the influence of Eliot in the early stages of writing 'Funland'. In his BBC Radio 3 introduction to the poem he makes particular reference to the lines from 'East Coker'

> *The whole earth is our hospital*
> *Endowed by the ruined millionaire.*

That sense of a fickle spirit, some 'wanton boy' using humanity for his 'sport', was behind the world of 'Funland'. In the Cedars asylum that

microcosm of the world is governed by the
doctors' authority, though for his brief periods
of supernatural power Pythagoras reigns in direct
descent from the great thinkers of antiquity. He
yields an ancient and occult force. However, like
Marlowe's Faustus, his power is ultimately no
more than a series of distractions. There are
tricks, but no miracles. Overturning the laws of
nature and questioning the authority of the
hospital staff, he is, in fact, doing little more than
gesturing.

His fellow patient Charlie dismisses him cynically
at the beginning of the play:

PYTHAGORAS: *Think blue, say green. And squeeze apple
pips from a tangerine. Ha, ha, ha.*
CHARLIE: *Music of the spheres, my foot. Like I said
to Dr Aquillus, you're just a second-class
stage magician with a paid-up Equity card
now in the bin with the rest of us.*

In one sense he is: in the real world he is. But
Pythagoras does not solely inhabit the real world,
he extends the confines of the hospital/world
and creates by his magic the means of escape.
Because Pythagoras is a rebel, dangerous in
thought and action, he attracts us. Wouldn't the
world, we wonder be a larger place if magical
vision were not proscribed by authority? What
would be the consequence of a life that gave full
rein to the imagination?

Sadly, but with a safe predictability, Pythagoras is
returned to the banality of the institutionalised
insane at the end of the play. This time when he

points at a telephone and it instantly rings the phenomenon is accepted as coincidence.

> (DR AQUILLUS puts down phone and laughs heartily. DR GREEN joins in laughter. But PYTHAGORAS puts down suitcase and sits down, evidently disturbed)

AQUILLUS: *It was just coincidence . . . that phone*

GREEN: *Are you all right Pythagoras?*

AQUILLUS: *Don't call him Pythagoras. His name is Tony Smith.*

PYTHAGORAS: *I'll just sit down a minute. I'll be all right in a sec.*

> (The snow outside descends across the window. Very faint now the distant carol can be heard again. Lights gradually down)

The spell, or whatever it was Pythagoras wove, is now broken. The snow and carols signal an accepted ritual rather than any miraculous birth. The play whimpers effectively to its close.

Those ideas about magic and medicine, poetry and prognosis, the rational and the irrational, are projected from the writer's own situation. Dannie Abse, when questioned about his poems, responds by saying:

They are the poems of a fortunate man.

The solid conviction of that reply rests on a complexity of events and issues. Dannie Abse's writing is successful because he can draw energy from a range of polarities: he is both a Welshman

60

and a Jew; a professional man of science and a
professional artist; a Londoner whose heart is in
Cardiff; he ran a chest clinic and at night was a
poetry and jazz performer; while he worked in
Soho, he lived in Golders Green. And so on:
Dannie Abse encloses in his life and art a set of
dualities. On several occasions he has talked of
being an outsider—yet he is a public figure broadcasting on television and radio regularly, and is
acting currently as the President of the Poetry
Society. Still, the earlier poems and, as I have
shown, the novel SOME CORNER OF AN ENGLISH
FIELD, are often concerned with the need to
establish an identity and to resolve paradoxes
within that identity.

Dannie Abse's development as a poet is that of a
writer who begins by rejoicing in the discovery
that he can sing and shout through his poems,
and then dedicates himself to testing this new-
found voice against the world. He tries it against
experiences in his life and in his reading, determined to prove that it is his own voice, the voice
through which his own life speaks.

To be accepted for publication by the reputable
Hutchinson & Co. while a student in his early
twenties was a notable achievement. It is a
measure of Dannie Abse's strength as a poet that
he quite quickly came to see the weaknesses of
that early work.

It is always difficult for a young poet to assess
himself. The context of established and fashionable writing is that body of work which defines
poetry for him. Yet how is one to find oneself in

the crammed wavelengths of all the other voices? In later years Dannie Abse was to call them, 'such noisy echoes'. When he began to write seriously in the 1940s, the dominant voices in English poetry were those of W. H. Auden and Dylan Thomas. The young Abse was sure to be susceptible to both influences. Auden's political and social concern and that of the other '30s 'Pink Poets' could easily take root in the background of left-wing commitment created in the Abse household, especially by brother Leo. Dylan Thomas was, at first, the outrageous iconoclast hitting London like a rocket from Wales, and later popularly characterised as the tragic young god sacrificed for Poetry. It may be argued that Dannie Abse was confronted by two of the most immediately persuasive poetic models of the century.

He began to write in 1941 while still at school. Leo had a copy of the anthology POEMS FOR SPAIN and in that book Dannie Abse discovered a form of writing which was quite distinct from that encountered in his school syllabus—Tennyson, and the Romantics.

Here I read for the first time poets whose adult moral concerns and protestations engaged my own wrath and indignation. Their voices had a passionate immediacy and their language was fresh, of the twentieth century. The raw political poems of the Spanish peasant poet, Miguel Hernandez, moved me to express my own indignation about the horrors of war in verse. I had begun to write verse voluntarily, not as an exercise for school. I hardly thought about technique at first or worried about owning a voice of my own.

Affected by the anger and involvement of these new poets, particularly Miguel Hernandez, Dannie Abse recognised that his own feelings of concern could, perhaps should, find expression through poetry. The Abse household was a supportive but challenging place, a fertile ground for thought and expression. The influence of Wilfred the medical student and Leo the orator was a challenge to complacency and offered models for positive action. At the same time there was the down-to-earth stability of his father's observations.

Young poets have to be seduced by words to commit themselves to poetry. It is at first dream, than a task and, perhaps, finally a dream again. That Dannie Abse would have 'caught, like an infection, the neo-Romantic fashionable mode of the time' may, in retrospect, seem inevitable. In the introduction to his COLLECTED POEMS he characterises those early poems as

so easy to write and so hard to read.

Only one poem from his first collection AFTER EVERY GREEN THING is included in the COLLECTED POEMS. 'The Uninvited' is evidence that this poet had real quality from the beginning.

> *They came into our lives unasked for.*
> *There was light momentarily, a flicker of wings,*
> *a dance, a voice, and then they went out*
> *again, like a light, leaving us not so much*
> *in darkness, but in a different place*
> *and alone as never before.*

It is an acknowledgement of responsibility, a recognition that one has to be open to other people. Our common humanity demands it. There is the paradox of discovery and loss. We discover that we are not alone, and thus lose our uniqueness.

> *So we have been changed*
> *and our vision no longer what it was,*
> *and our hopes no longer what they were;*
> *so a piece of us has gone out with them also,*
> *a cold dream subtracted without malice,*
>
> *the weight of another world added also,*

The tone is enquiring, the pace firm and the diction clean and direct. The irresistible intrusion, and thus association, is strange and wonderful:

> *We did not beckon them in, they came in uninvited,*
> *the sunset pouring from their shoulders.*

There is a transference of the burden of living, a sharing of responsibility too. Some sort of baptism has taken place,

> *so they walked through us as they would through water*

As one might expect, Dannie Abse was ready to become involved in the philosophy of the individual predicament.

> *. . . in the 1950's I was interested in existentialist literature, in Sartre and Camus, and how they dramatised philosophical questions.*

64

His second book, WALKING UNDER WATER, appeared in 1952 and brought together poems from the previous three years. The influences evident in AFTER EVERY GREEN THING are still present, but there are several notable accomplishments in the finished pieces. The collection includes 'Song for Dov Shamir', the 'translation' that had drawn a compliment from Eliot, and the lyrical 'Epithalamion', which over the years has continued to attract anthologists.

> *Singing, today I married my white girl*
> *beautiful in a barley field.*
> *Green on thy finger a grass blade curled,*
> *so with this ring I thee wed, I thee wed,*
> *and send our love to the loveless world*
> *of all the living and all the dead.*

There is an unrestrained romanticism, progressing by repetition and rhyme, calling on associations from fertility myth and the Pastoral. The sheer ebullience of the piece ensures that all but the most niggardly, ice-bound critic will be carried along in the celebration. The Keatsian *unloads its liquid cargoes/of marigolds*; the awkwardness of the first three lines of the second stanza; the Dylanesque *all the living and the dead*—these are transparently unoriginal, and yet the whole thing is carried off with a confident energy.

In other poems in this book one hears quite a different voice. 'Letter to Alex Comfort' and 'Portrait of a Marriage', both included in the COLLECTED POEMS, are cooler pieces. Here the rhyme-schemes emphasise a more analytical or polemic intent.

'Portrait of a Marriage' proceeds to dissect the banality of a tired, 'suburban' relationship that has exhausted its life. The yellow fullness of 'barley' in 'Epithalamion' is immediately excluded by the return again

> To the suburban house

and the woman's escape into romantic novels produced by a

> million edition pen

Until

> untamed voices

can rise through

> the civilised bore

until she and her husband can voice this predicament to each other, she will continue to hide herself behind the illusion of normality:

> the cut-glass vases you endow
> with flowers, to disguise this here and now.

Cut flowers are a poor substitute for the

> gold af barley

This poem is a significant inclusion in WALKING UNDER WATER. It counterpoints the lushness of many of the other poems in the book. In lines such as

> *You dare not entertain*
> *questions like—Can I start again? Seek divorce?*

and an image such as

> *in the stabbed evenings*

the influence of T. S. Eliot's early work, 'The Love-Song of J. Alfred Prufrock especially, has replaced that of Dylan Thomas.

To label 'Letter to Alex Comfort' as Audenesque would be simplistic, however. The poem is best understood as a celebration of a fellow practitioner—in both medicine and poetry—and through that, a consideration of the two dominant factors they share. This poem represents the clearest early attempt by the poet to analyse the nature of his art and its place in his life, for several important distinctions are made. Dannie Abse sees in Alex Comfort a mirror-image of himself: both men wear the

> *white coat and purple coat*

Abse sends wishes of success to Comfort in his research:

> *Alex, perhaps a colour of which neither of us had dreamt*
> *may appear in the test-tube with God knows what admonition.*

But this is not to be won at the price of the corruption of the spirit. He fears that the imagination may be weighed down or worn thin by the necessary attrition of the laboratory. Dannie Abse is highly sceptical of *true German thoroughness*

and with good reason. His treatment of Germany and Germans over the years needs further attention. I shall return to this later.

In the present poem the solid German research of Koch and Ehrlich is set unfavourably against the everyday, human context of other discoveries such as those of Newton who

> *leaning in Woolsthorpe against the garden wall*
> *forgot his indigestion and all such trivialities,*
> *but gaped up at heaven in just surprise, and, with*
> *true gravity, witnessed the vertical apple fall.*

Or Archimedes,

That Greek one, then, is my hero who watched the bath water
rise above his navel, and rushed out naked, 'I found it,
I found it' into the street in all his shining and forgot
that others would only stare at his genitals.
   What laughter!

At least with such

> *a pedestrian miracle*

as these, the poet feels, there is also a celebration of the human random or contingent experience. As he says in his interview with Joseph Cohen, in 1982,

My consciousness of recent history: the nuclear crimes in
Nagasaki, Hiroshima; the crimes of Auschwitz, Dachau;
the geography of Vietnapalm; awful opening mouths of the

68

lethal crowd; this awareness does not diminish with the years.
On the contrary.

As a man of science, and as a Jew, living in the immediate post-war period he has a heightened awareness of the consequences of cold, logical thought, of scientific developments untempered by human feelings. This poem argues the human case as his best plays would in later years.

The poet, in his affection for Alex Comfort, is celebrating those who dig deep

into the wriggling earth for a rainbow with an honest spade.

He curses

> *those clever scientists*
> *who dissect away the wings and haggard heart from*
> *the dove.*

It may be objected that the vision of

> *the unkempt*
> *voyagers who, like butterflies drunk with suns,*
> *can only totter crookedly in the dazed air*
> *to reach, charmingly, their destination as if by accident*

is just another neo-Romantic, bohemian posture, but I think it has a more lasting significance than that. Dannie Abse's poetry matures steadily; he focuses on the particular; encourages suspicion of the system and argues for tolerance of the unconventional. One approaches the eccentric not condemning, but rather, asking what the experience might teach one. Science and logic are not the only roads to truth. Can we be sure that they form the most direct vision? The purple coat may wear as well as the white coat. As Keats observed, *I do not see how truth is to be arrived at by the process of logical thought.*

TENANTS OF THE HOUSE, Abse's third collection, published in 1957, brings together poems from the first half of that decade and signals a distinctly new voice. Dannie Abse has by this time developed a style that is able to articulate his concern for a post-war world that seems to be losing its way. There is a new strangeness in these poems: most of the characters who appear are confused, displaced or doomed. In a succession of allegories one finds echoes of the existentialist warnings projected from the other side of the English Channel.

The collection opens as if Dannie Abse were stating his intention to move on as a poet. 'Leaving Cardiff' introduces the idea of movement and discovery that is worked into the allegorical 'The Mountaineers'. However, there is still a subscription here to the Romantic ideal of suffering creativity, following in the footsteps of Shakespeare, Milton and Wordsworth—

> *Still we climb to the chandelier stars*
> *and the more we sing the more we die.*

but the focus returns finally to the individual writer making his own way, paying his own dues,

> *We discovered more than footprints in the snow,*
> *more than mountain ghost, more than desolate glory,*

70

yet now, looking down, we see nothing below
except wind, steaming ice, floating mist—and so
silently, sadly, we follow higher the rare songs of oxygen.
The more we climb the further we have to go.

That recognition of the task ahead is wittily underpinned by his 'Letter to The Times' in which he logically dismantles the Romantic aesthetic, particularly the centrality of the pathetic fallacy.

You can't trust a star, that's sure.
So when the greenfly is in the rose,
and the dragonfly drops its shadow in the river;
when the axe hides in the tree with its listening
shriek, and clouds gag the starlight
with grey handkerchiefs—I contend, Sir,
that we should pity them no more,
but concern ourselves with more natural things.

As Pope said, *The proper study of Mankind is Man.* Dannie Abse's poetry over the following thirty years consistently, perhaps exclusively, concerns itself with man. For Abse the natural world is unique and compelling because it has man at its centre. Ten years after 'Letter to The Times' he answers an imaginary questioner after a poetry reading:

Yes, madam, as a poet I do take myself seriously,
and since I have a young, questioning family, I suppose
I should know something about English wild flowers:

yet he finally admits:

> *But no! Done for in the ignorant suburb,*
> *I'll drink Scotch, neurotically stare through glass*
> *at the rainy lawn, at green stuff, nameless birds,*
> *and let my daughter, madam, go to nature class.*
> *I'll not compete with those nature poets you advance,*
> *some in country dialect, and some in dialogue*
> *with the country—few as calm as their words:*
> *Wordsworth, Barnes, sad John Clare who ate grass.*

'As I was saying' is, again, a witty, serious statement of intent. Dannie Abse cannot compete with the great nature poets, nor does he wish to. Those poets are major thinkers because it is themselves, man, which they elucidate through experience in nature. Abse is urban; he is in his natural environment in the middle of the twentieth century and therefore must record and explain the human condition in that context.

In TENANTS OF THE HOUSE he is clearly developing new poetic strategies in order to achieve this. In 'Duality', 'The Trial', 'Emperors of the Island', 'New Babylons', 'The Meeting' and several others, he makes palpable the mid-century crises. These poems demand our commitment—think, decide, they say, otherwise you cannot claim to exist in any meaningful way, and, in any case, you may not survive. The best of these political poems have a sad relevance for us still. At the crossroads of the century which way does one turn?

> *Each would go their separate ways*
> *as the East or the West wind blows—*
> *and dark and light they both would praise.*
> *but one would melt, the other one freeze.*

So many masks have been worn that the human face may no longer recognise itself—

> *Now, now, I hang these masks on the wall.*
> *Oh Christ, take one and leave me all*
> *lest four tears from two eyes fall.*

These *existentialist ballads*, as Joseph Cohen (THE POETRY OF DANNIE ABSE) has called them, have a cumulative energy that develops through this collection, pinning the individual down like Prufrock's moth, persistently involving the reader in that process of self-scrutiny.

> *With the wrong mask, another man's life I live—*
> *I must seek my own face, find my own grave.*
>
> ('The Trial')

These are uncomfortable poems for the reader and there seems nowhere to escape. Even two poems of married life, 'Verses at Night' and 'The Moment', are disturbed by nightmare—

> *What are you thinking? Do you love me?*
>
> *Suddenly you are not you at all but a ghost*
> *dreaming of a castle to haunt or a heavy garden;*
> *some place eerie, and far from me. But now a door is*
> *banging outside, so you turn your head surprised.*
>
> *You speak my name and someone else has died.*

We delude ourselves if we think that we can secure ourselves against the tides of loss and pain. We are all

> *Out on the tormented, midnight sea.*

73

each trying to stay afloat, and love is the only way to touch another.

> *And I call your name as loud as I can*
> *and I give you all the light I am.*

As in 'A Night Out' from A SMALL DESPERATION the marital bed is the microcosm, the brief glimpse of a perfect world that eclipses

> *. . . the spotlight drama of our nightmares;*
> *images of Auschwitz almost authentic,*

As tenants, the responsibility for maintaining the house rests with each one of us. 'Social Revolution in England' argues that our traditional masters, the hereditary lords of the land, are no longer in touch. When the revolutionaries rampage through their houses they can do no more than cough discreetly and stand aside.

There is little likelihood either of divine intervention. Should our saviour make his second coming he would probably die unnoticed:

> *He cannot rise further.*
> *The earth is heavy on his shoulders.*
> *Cry out, shout, oh help is near.*
> *Dangerously, the machine passes scything corn,*
> *but the driver does not hear, cannot hear*
> *—and now that noble head is gone,*
> *a liquid redness in the yellow*
> *where the mouth had been.*

'The Second Coming' places Dannie Abse nearer to Ted Hughes than to W. B. Yeats. The violent death is arbitrary, but still encoded in Nature:

74

> *Dig, I say dig, you'll*
> *find arms, lions, white legs, to prove my story—*
> *and one red poppy in the corn.*

That is a striking image, bringing the reader to
focus on the actual. In the choice of the poppy
this poem moves from being a general con-
demnation of human indifference and insen-
sitivity to cite the dead of two world wars.
The ghosts of the war dead and our debt to them
are referred to again in 'The Meeting'

> *Far away the conscripted dead, the scarecrow in the dark*
> *field, like an artificial ragged ghost.*

Allegorical pieces such as these are much more
successful than the directly referential poem 'The
Victim of Aulis' which treats of Agamemnon's
decision to sacrifice Iphigeneia at the instigation
of Calchas, the official soothsayer. The bare
narrative of a poem like 'Emperors of the Island'
has a greater strength; it has the universality of
parable. Indeed, Dannie Abse labels the piece, *a
political parable to be read aloud*. One thinks of William
Golding's castaways on his nightmare coral
island and the seeming inevitability of jealousy,
greed and suspicion committing man to self-
destruction. The poet avoids slogans or specific
political targets; he does not name names, but
draws the reader into the chilling rhythm of the
murders. It remains one of the most enduring
poems from the Cold War years, the beginning
of our 'Bomb Culture'.

The spilt yolk image that was used to good effect
in 'The Second Coming' is seen again in 'Elegy

for Dylan Thomas'. Written a few weeks after the
poet's death in the November of 1953, this piece
is an unrestrained celebration of the man and his
style.

All down the valleys they are talking,
and in the community of the smoke-laden town
Tomorrow, through bird trailed skies, across labouring waves,
wrong-again Emily will come to the dandelion yard
and, with rum tourists, inspect his grave.

The poem develops as a recognition of Thomas's
personal feelings and sees that he will become the
victim of anecdotal remembrances:

Too familiar you blaspheme his name and collected legends.

But the poem ends with a real sympathy for
Dylan, an ocean away from Wales and home.
Dylan who was spilled carelessly by death.

Stranger, he is laid to rest
not in the nightingale dark nor in the canary light.
At the dear last, the yolk broke in his head,
blood of his soul's egg in a splash of bright
voices and now he is dead.

This was one of the better elegies for Dylan (and
there were dozens of memorial poems published
at that time) but in terms of Dannie Abse's work
it can also be read as an elegy for the influence of
Dylan Thomas on his style. The parable, the
poetic sensibility in an urban landscape, these are
to be the cornerstones of the poet's future work.
After involving us as TENANTS OF THE HOUSE, he
ensures that the location of that house for him

76

is clear. His next book is entitled POEMS, GOLDERS GREEN.

The elegy for Dylan was one of three poems in Dannie Abse's third book concerned with, or set in, Wales. There are fewer and fewer such pieces in the collections that follow. The occasional childhood recollection and the treatment of the death of his father in Llandough are among his best-received work, but Dannie Abse, apart from retaining his well-used season ticket in the Ninian Park stand for Cardiff City's matches, settles into the environment of London both as a doctor and as a poet.

In the London of the mid-1950s Dannie Abse was drawn into what might now be viewed as one of the minor personality crises in English poetics. Whilst he was trying to balance his own poetic ideas against the influence of his fellow-countryman Thomas, there were a number of poets and magazines in strident reaction against what they considered to be the excesses of Dylan. They saw him as either erring to the Romantic extreme or to the surreal extreme.

The writing of poetry has always been a solitary business (North American creative writing courses apart) but the arguments that arise later about what has been written or what one should be writing often intrigue poets and poetasters alike. When Anthony Hartley wrote in THE SPECTATOR in 1954 that a new wave of poets was emerging to lead English verse away from the esoteric excesses of the neo-Romantic 1940s, his view was taken up like a banner.

77

For better or worse we are now in the presence of the only considerable movement in English poetry since the 'thirties.

The 'Movement' it was to be then, and it swept along poets as various as Philip Larkin, John Wain, Elizabeth Jennings and Thom Gunn. These writers, together with Amis and Davie, were collected in the most influential anthology of the decade: NEW LINES, edited by Robert Conquest in 1956.

The book seemed to proclaim a sensible, robust, pragmatic approach to the brave new post-war world. As Ian Hamilton has said ('The Making of the Movement' in BRITISH POETRY SINCE 1960, ed. Schmidt):

They had rediscovered irony, wit and syntax, they bowed the knee to Leavis, Empson and Orwell. More than all this, though, they represented in their verse moral attitudes which were excitingly appropriate to the grey new Britain of the 'fifties'.

In literature, as in politics, one orthodoxy fades only for another to rise. Bearing in mind the poems in TENANTS OF THE HOUSE, one could not be surprised that Dannie Abse's natural inclination was to resist the fashionable labelling of poets in this way. In 'New Babylons' he plainly states his position:

> *Time's fires leap and burn*
> *and mavericks such as I*
> *must be branded in their turn—*
> *to reek of human flesh*
> *whilst venal courtiers cry:*
> *'Conform, conform or die.'*

He wants to be counted with the mavericks, each holding to his own notion of the

> . . . *timeless honesties*

The immediate targets of 'New Babylons' are authoritarian acts of government, here and in other countries, and the only defence is to humour one's own beliefs.

> *When Nebuchadnezzars rage*
> *no maverick is immune*
> *for it's we, ourselves, who cry:*
> *'Conform, conform and die.'*

So must it be with writing. In 1957 Dannie Abse co-edited MAVERICKS (with Howard Sergeant, whose maverick magazine OUTPOSTS continues strongly into the 1980s).

This alternative anthology, published under the imprint of Abse's own POETRY AND POVERTY magazine press, was a calculated blow against the new establishment. It was a collection of some quality which included Jon Silkin and Vernon Scannell, and though now, a quarter of a century later, the significance of MAVERICKS seems minor, it was at the time a strongly felt gesture in the context of 'The Movement' and the subsequent debate.

A 'Maverick' quality colours so much of Dannie Abse's poetry: he embodies, after all, such a complexity of identities that he was bound to oppose the idea that poets are susceptible to classification. As the influence of Dylan Thomas waned, it becomes less and less helpful to call Abse an Anglo-Welsh poet; no more help, certainly, than to call him an Anglo-Jewish poet.

The sense of a need to establish an identity that informs poems such as 'The Trial', 'Duality' and 'New Babylons' finds a more direct expression in POEMS, GOLDERS GREEN. At home

> *It's unusual to meet a beggar,*
> *you hardly ever see a someone drunk.*
> *It's a nice, clean, quiet, religious place.*
> *For my part, now and then, I want to scream:*
> *thus, by the neighbours, am considered odd.*

whilst in the sleazy district in which Dannie Abse's chest clinic is located,

> *It's customary to see many beggars,*
> *common to meet people roaring and drunk.*
> *It's a nice, loud, dirty, irreligious place.*
> *For my part, now and then, I want to scream:*
> *thus, by Soho friends, am considered odd.*

The poet seems destined to feel 'odd', out of place. As he was 'Leaving Cardiff' in the previous collection there seemed to be a promise of fulfilment. Experience has now brought him to the realisation that things are more complex than that: fulfilment is not a place you can aim for. In his 'Return to Cardiff' he confronts the need to locate himself; a need which he has carried with him.

> *Unable to define anything I can hardly speak,*
> *and still I love the place for what I wanted it to be*

> *as much as for what it unashamedly is*
> *now for me, a city of strangers, alien and bleak.*

He is the first to admit the inevitable distortions
wrought by memory and need:

> *. . . the boy I was not and the man I am not*
> *met, hesitated, left double footsteps, then walked on.*

One does not find oneself, ever. Life is the process
of composing oneself, and for Dannie Abse the
poetry and autobiographical writings are at the
centre of that need; the means and the end of
that quest.

Three poems—'After the Release of Ezra Pound',
'Red Balloon' and 'Postmark'—fix at the centre
of the collection the poet as a Jew. Because he is
a Jew Dannie Abse cannot excuse the great poet
Pound, who was an anti-semitic collaborator. He
became a passionate supporter of Mussolini's
fascist Italy and acted for the Italians as a 'Lord
Haw-Haw', broadcasting fascist propaganda
across Europe. Pound's noise was one of the
ugliest sounds from Abse's childhood. After the
fall of Italy he was captured by the Allies and was
under threat of execution as a traitor, but T. S.
Eliot, on whose 'Waste Land' Pound had been
such a guiding influence, raised a petition of
eminent writers to plead for leniency. I remember
Vernon Watkins telling me that he had signed;
many of his peers did too, and Pound was saved
from the hangman. He was consigned instead to
an 'asylum' and lived there in comparative ease.

In the spring of 1958 Pound emerged and for most people he figured, if at all, as a curiosity.

> In the beer and espresso bars they talked
> of Ezra Pound, excusing the silences of an old man,
> saying there is so little time between
> the parquet floors of an institution
> and the boredom of the final box.

However, as a poet and as a Jew, Abse cannot condone Pound's seeming intransigency.

> Why, Paul, if that tickling distance between
> was merely a journey long enough
> to walk the circumference of a Belsen,
> Walt Whitman would have been eloquent,
> and Thomas Jefferson would have cursed.

Pound fails as a poet and as a man, creatively and morally, if he cannot redeem his gross error in aiding the cause that sent millions of Jews, gypsies, homosexuals, Jehovah's Witnesses and many other minorities to the death camps and the gas chambers.

Dannie Abse, like Harold Pinter and Arnold Wesker, is conscious of the implicit threat of anti-semitism in his childhood. His experiences were never as direct or traumatic as theirs—Pinter sees the roots of his characters' violence in his victimisation as a child in London's East End —but in the bizarrely phallic 'Red Balloon' and, more successfully, in 'Postmark', Dannie Abse does deal with the special threat to him as a Jew.

In writing about Sylvia Plath recently ('The Dread of Sylvia Plath' in the small magazine SEA

LEGS No. 1 June 1983) Dannie Abse shows himself to be very conscious of the dangers implicit in using material from the Holocaust. He points out the

larger moral dilemma which exercises critics, that dilemma which inheres in George Steiner's powerful question: 'In what sense does anyone, himself uninvolved and long after the event, commit a subtle larceny when he invokes the echoes and trappings of Auschwitz and appropriates an enormity of ready emotion to his own private design?'

Whilst being sympathetic towards the predicament of the self-tortured Plath, Dannie Abse is wary of the manipulation of the historical fact and the internalised horror. One invokes the memory of the Holocaust for its own sake, to inform and remind us all of the depths in our shared heart of darkness. The appropriation of those images, those bestial facts, to our own sufferings may well be a reduction, an insult to the collective memory.

'The Dread of Sylvia Plath' raises essential questions about the nature of the poem when it involves uniquely personal dilemmas. Building on a quotation from the American critic M. L. Rosenthal, Dannie Abse discusses the nature of the 'Confessional Poet':

M. L. Rosenthal invented the useful term 'Confessional Poet' to categorise those, like Plath, who broadcast the drama of their disordered emotional life and made their 'Psychological vulnerability and shame' an embodiment of our history and civilisation. This is quite different from being simply an autobiographical poet who, to quote another American,

Daniel Hoffman, is not 'trapped by emotional illness, in sufferings brought on by unresolvable crises.' He is able to 'use more of his life in his work and even when the poet's subject is similar to the confessional poet's, that subject may be viewed with perspective, detachment, humour.' In short, the unhealthy confessional poet, compared with the healthy auto-biographical one, is likely to be much more limited. Who can dispute that? All the same, the jet-energy force of a poetry like that of Sylvia Plath's resides precisely in this very same narrowness of bore.

Once more the argument leads back to individual responsibility. This writer addresses himself time and time again to that question. Perhaps with the weight of the recent past as his special burden, a Jew hears the question more insistently.

When his father lies dying 'In Llandough Hospital' the images which strike Dannie Abse are significant:

> *Now since death makes victims of us all,*
> *he's thin as Auschwitz in that bed.*

Unlike Sylvia Plath, Dannie Abse has a legitimate claim on the image. His sorrow and anger at the impending loss of his father occasion the comparison with the ultimate shared suffering. The ungrammatical use of 'Auschwitz' goes beyond the language of the ordinary: it has indeed become a name with profound resonances. His father is as thin as if he had been victim of the camp, but

> *Still his courage startles me. The fears*
> *I'd have, he has none. Who'd save*

84

Socrates from the hemlock,
or Winkelreid from the spears?

We quote or misquote in defeat,
in life, and at the camps of death.
Here comes the night with all its stars,
bright butchers' hooks for man and meat.

That's such a forceful image that the remaining
two stanzas pose questions that have been
rendered redundant.

'In Llandough Hospital' appeared in A SMALL
DESPERATION. The next collection FUNLAND contains 'No More Mozart' which is Abse's most
enraged comment on the Holocaust and the
irredeemable guilt of the Germans.

The very landscape of Germany is charged with
militarism,

High to the right a hill of trees
a fuselage of branches
reflects German moonlight
like dull armour.
Sieg heil!

The poem, written on a visit to that country in
1970, is a catalogue of nightmarish associations

Now, of course, no more Mozart.
With eyes closed still
the body touches itself, takes stock.
Above the hands the thin wrists
attached to them; and on the wrists
the lampshade material.
Also the little hairs that can be pulled.

85

> *The eyes open:*
> *the German earth is made of helmets;*
> *the wind seeps through a deep*
> *frost hole that is somewhere else*
> *carrying the far Jew-sounds of railway trucks.*

The strength and persistence of the anger in this poem fulfil Dannie Abse's own prescription in 'Not Beautiful' from his previous book. While admiring the saintly qualities of forgiveness and celebration—

> *In all hiroshimas, in raw and raving voices,*
> *live skeletons of the Camp, flies hugging faeces,*
> *in war, in famine, he'd find the beautiful.*

Abse also recognises the legitimacy, the purity of anger:

> *One sees the good point, of course, and may admire it;*
> *but, sometimes, I think that to curse is more sacred*
> *than to pretend by affirming. And offend.*

'No More Mozart' is by far his most successful poetic attempt to deal with the Holocaust. I have already drawn attention to 'A Night Out' from A SMALL DESPERATION. Those celluloid images raised by

> *. . . the new Polish film*
> *at the Academy in Oxford Street*

are surely too horrific though for us to believe that the Abses

. . . watched, as we munched milk chocolate,
trustful children, no older than our own,
strolling into the chambers without fuss,
whilst smoke, black and curly, oozed from chimneys.

The closing image of marital love is undercut by the heavy, perhaps clumsy, irony of their return-ing home to the reassuring smile of

. . . the au pair girl from Germany

The whole poem is an attack on that apparent sense of security offered by life in

. . . the comfortable suburb

Such a life can dull one's responses, blunt one's anger, and Dannie Abse takes every opportunity to shake the foundations of suburban living. 'A Night Out' affirms the power of marital love, but it also warns against living entirely in one's own life. Their love-making is a positive emotional response to the events of that evening, but it cannot change anything.

In Sidney Lumet's fine film 'The Pawnbroker' the death camp survivor, played by Rod Steiger, is constantly reminded of and terrified by those parallels with the Nazi horrors which he sees around him in the streets of New York. He is a broken man but the memories give him a uniquely clear perspective in the city's shadows. Those memories finally save his soul. Dannie Abse, too, realises that we need the nightmares —they morally inform us.

In his most recent collection, WAY OUT IN THE
CENTRE, he has a poem which recreates a similar
situation. 'Another Street Scene (Outside the
grocer's, Golders Green Road)' describes a public
quarrel between a black-bearded man and his
wife. They are arguing about the raising of their
son. The man quotes the Talmud, his wife flies at
him in a rage. It's an odd incident, unexplained
and apparently unresolved, except that the anger
generated between the two of them somehow
raises for the man a disturbing spectre:

> The bearded man has closed his eyes.
> Who's this, disguised as a beggar,
> playing a violin without strings?
>
> What music's this, its cold measure?
> Who are these, dangling from lampposts,
> kicking as if under water?

That image of war, of pogroms, touches the
collective subconscious of Europe, and so it
should. This poem has much in common with
the earlier 'My Uncle Isidore' from 'New Poems'
in the COLLECTED POEMS. The bearded uncle,
however, plays his violin as a means of supplica-
tion to the God who saw Auschwitz and
Treblinka built. Isidore is an occasional visitor,
very much the figure of European Jewry—strange
and foreign to the Cardiff Abse. And yet Dannie
Abse, though removed from that aspect of his
life, wants to celebrate the special nature of that
heritage.

> I think of Uncle Isidore—smelly
> schnorrer and lemon-tea bolshevik—my foreign
> distant relative, not always distant.

The adolescent Abse in ASH ON A YOUNG MAN'S
SLEEVE comes to see that to understand his own
position he must associate in spirit with the Jews
in Europe. However, in 'Tales from Shatz' in the
COLLECTED POEMS he deals with the pressures
upon British Jews to mask themselves and
become absorbed into the main body of society.

> *Consider the mazzle of Baruch Levy*
> *who changed his name to Barry Lee,*
> *who moved to Esher, Surrey,*
> *who sent his four sons—Matthew, Mark*
> *Luke and John—to boarding school,*
> *who had his wife's nose fixed,*
> *who, blinking in the Gents,*
> *turned from the writing on the wall*
> *and later, still blinking, joined the golf club.*

During a round of golf with 'Colonel Owen' a
storm erupts and the Colonel is struck dead by
lightning. This is not as disastrous as Barry Lee
thinks at first for he discovers that the Colonel

> *once was known as Moshe Cohen.*

Dannie Abse ensures that he does not commit
the errors of Sylvia Plath. Plath's humour is too
rare, too black; it even has the strange effect of
diminishing her own position. Pieces flake off her
at every laugh. Abse's humour is that of the wry
anecdote. In his most recent collection, three
poems—'Of Rabbi Yose', 'Snake' and 'Of Itzig and
his Dog'—continue that strategy. The story has
elements of parable: it will probably hinge on an
aphoristic remark, a wry, witty saying. So, from
the Torah Rabbi Yose attempts to explicate

> *'Thou shalt grope at noonday*
> *as the blind gropeth in darkness.'*

and again the Rabbi Hanina ben Dosa, who, as tradition has it, was bitten by a snake, finds that the snake dies. Learned men ponder these mysteries, for

> *Remember, he who has been bitten*
> *by a snake thereafter becomes*
> *frightened of a rope . . .*

Such poems argue that insight is in narrative, and wisdom in the substance of language. The story-form releases a knowledge more vital, more accessible than that encoded in chemical definitions:

> *Now, tonight, a clean-shaven rabbi*
> *who once studied in Vienna*
> *says snake-venom contains*
>
> *haemolysins, haemo-*
> *coagulants, protolysins,*
> *cytolysins and neurotoxins*

Between the associations that the human mind composes—the snake really being, after all,

> *a penis, an unruly penis*
> *making a noise like one pissing*
> *on a mound of fresh hot ashes.*

—and the application of traditional scholarship, one may find the truth.

Dannie Abse raids Talmudic and Chasidic sources for some of his poems, but that should be set in the wider context of his use of other traditions, from the classical origins of 'Victim of Aulis' and 'Funland' to the most recent appropriation of a Bushmen legend—'The Young Man and the Lion' and a Native American song, 'The Bad Boy of the North-West Coast'.

Nevertheless, it is his discovered sense of his own Jewishness that motivates so many of his poems. John Pikoulis (in POETRY WALES October 1977) has argued that this commitment is an uneasy response and that here lies the central dilemma for Dannie Abse. Pikoulis traces it from ASH ON A YOUNG MAN'S SLEEVE through to the later work. He attributes the shortcomings of SOME CORNER OF AN ENGLISH FIELD and O. JONES, O. JONES to the appropriateness of the author's identification with, respectively, Henderson and Ozymandias. He sees the Romantic poetry of the immediate post-war years as an objective correlative to the revelations of the Holocaust and their author's own spiritual and emotional involvement with these.

In POET IN THE FAMILY Dannie Abse states clearly

I often think of my not going to Belsen

However, I think Pikoulis too neat in his explanation. Abse's poetry does more than create *an imagined Jewishness*. It is clear now that there are more direct references to the Jewish heritage than those which Pikoulis mentioned. *The poetry of his sad predicament* is not just a product of his emerging need to establish an identity as a Jew. It is more complex than that. There is a range of paradoxes in Dannie Abse and his work.

A healthy balance to Pilkoulis's view is that suggested by another article in that 1977 issue of POETRY WALES, this time by the Anglo-Welsh poet John Tripp. Tripp is positive in his praise of a fellow practitioner—

There are few contemporary practitioners in English who communicate such a sense of something very nasty continuing through us and around us—a sort of disquieting apprehension that things are about to fall apart even in the most banal and humdrum circumstances. It is as if he really wishes to celebrate only the spontaneous joys, the hopes and consolations of living, but is overtaken by his knowledge of the dust we each come to. Gently, tenderly, compassionately he reminds us— in sadness and some wonder—of the common fate.

By stressing the elements of experience and compassion which cross racial or religious differences, rather than the particularly Jewish influences, Tripp locates the poetic strengths of a man who is *Both fascinated and appalled by our slow, pitiful decay.*

In A SMALL DESPERATION and the books that follow Abse is often concerned with that decay and the way in which we have to confront the world while we are in possession of that knowledge. Probably the most famous poem from A SMALL DESPERATION is 'Pathology of colours'. It is a shocking confrontation with the facts of death and decomposition. Our conventional associations of colours are steadily, relentlessly opposed by harsher truths:

> *I know the colour rose, and it is lovely,*
> *but not when it ripens in a tumour;*
> *and healing greens, leaves and grass, so springlike*
> *in limbs that fester are not springlike.*

Each of the four stanzas has a concluding couplet that repeats, rhymes or para-rhymes, locking in the argument, reinforcing the bluntness of the paradox: for every beauty there is a grim equivalent.

Duality is at the core of so much that this writer does; he charts his progress through life, changing, developing as he moves into mature adulthood, yet always aware of the given facts of his own life, his roots in Wales and as a Jew. The world through which he moves reveals itself in more complex and ambiguous forms. The hazy, wordy images that fill the pages of AFTER EVERY GREEN THING dissolve and reform into a clearer and often more chilling vision. What appears now as an overblown stance in the first collection—

> *What shadow in the wind, the last hour of the sunflower*
> *flickering with pain of blackbirds and coffins,*
> *married her to the white flaming nails of Night?*
> *Against what cross of stars, her feet chained*
> *to the chanting ghosts, was she crucified,*
> *her sweet name maimed forever with the buried angel?*
>
> ('If the Dead Offend')

has, over twenty years, resolved itself into a more natural voice which is, on the whole, steady and firm, quietly insisting that we confront and answer the question of our mortality.

> *So in the simple blessing of a rainbow,*
> *in the bevelled edge of a sunlit mirror,*
> *I have seen, visible, Death's artefact*
> *like a soldier's ribbon on a tunic tacked.*

The challenge is to affirm life when all around one there are Death's emblems.

His father's illness and subsequent death focussed his vision more acutely at this time than ever before. 'In Llandough Hospital' records the last anguish of the dying; the desire to cling on to life and, at the same time, the obvious fact that in the face of extreme suffering

> *To hasten night would be humane*

Dannie Abse is rendered childlike by this most personal of hospital deaths,

> *So like a child I question why*
> *night with stars, then night without end.*

He carries 'Two Small Stones' away from his father's grave. In the face of death small gestures may hold the key to one's integrity, even one's sanity.

Our living challenges us to make sense of life: absurd though it may at times seem, we have no choice but to 'Hunt the thimble'. It is a game we enact with our lives and when we are close to discovery the full irony in which we are trapped is revealed:

Like those old men in hospital dying,
who, unaware strangers stand around their bed,
stare obscurely, for a long moment,
at one of their own hands raised—
which perhaps is bigger than the moon again—
and then, drowsy, wandering, shout out, 'Mama'.

Is it like that? Or hours after that even:
the darkness inside a dead man's mouth?

No, no, I have told you:
you are cold, and you cannot describe it.

The desperation Dannie Abse feels at this time
may be rooted in small incidents but it is persistent. In 'Olfactory Pursuits'

A man sniffs the back of his own hand,
moistens it with his mouth, to sniff again,
to think a blank; writes, 'The odour of stones.'

One is reminded of King Lear and his comment,
It smells of mortality. Stones fill a landscape of
despair which nature cannot soften: an attractive
girl encountered at a station that is 'Not
Adlestrop' is whisked away by her train's
'atrocious speed' with a movement that drowns
all possibility of Edward Thomas's singing birds;
this is a landscape that contains 'the sheds'
packed with the nightmares of recent history; a
landscape in which

sad John Clare . . . ate grass.

The suburbs offer a fragile, illusory sense of
security that might at any time be shattered by

. . . many stones, boulders even leaping down
out of earshot, down the sides of hell.
('A suburban episode')

Even the attempt to escape to 'A winter convalescence' leaves one at night in a strange, hotel bed, knowing that

> *The dark comes from the lift-shaft.*

In such a landscape of the 'Not beautiful' one may well do best to 'curse and offend'. Certainly, organised religions offer no more than

> *scrubbed, excremental visions*
> ('Even')

A desperate 'Interview with a spirit healer' may lead to

> *. . . but a sign ethereal as a psalm.*

All this is distilled into 'The motto'. And the motto is simply—

> *Be visited, expect nothing, and endure*

Encountering such relentless adversity, whatever can we stack against the trickling avalanche of small desperations?

For all its grim concern, A SMALL DESPERATION ends with a long poem of affirmation. 'The smile was' continues to engage the fact of mortality but is prepared to celebrate.

Never,
not for one single death
can I forget we die with the dead,
and the world dies with us;
yet
in one, lonely,
small child's birth
all the tall dead rise
to break the crust of the imperative earth.

It is as if the Yeatsian idea of gaiety from 'Lapis Lazuli' were transposed into the 'open field' American poetry of the mid-century. The structure of this poem appears to compose the poet's thoughts as it progresses to a definition at least, if not to a resolution, of the dilemma which hangs between a shooting star and the surgeon's smile. The human smile is positive, it propagates and liberates:

They all, still, smile like that,
when the child first whimpers like a seagull
the ancient smile reasserts itself
instinct with a return
so outrageous and so shameless;
always the same
> > *an uncaging*
> > *a freedom.*

A poetic resolution is still being reached for in the next collection, which comes to its climax in the title poem 'Funland'. The book has central poems such as 'No more Mozart' and 'In the theatre', but there's a growing indication of the poet's awareness that he is, now, following the death of his father, moving into his own middle years.

Some of the poems in FUNLAND are as close as Dannie Abse gets to writing 'confessional' poetry. Certainly there is a determined rooting to the actual:

> *. . . I start with the visible*
> *and am startled by the visible*
> ('Mysteries')

'A new diary' and 'Portrait of the artist as a middle-aged man' show him taking stock—at precisely 3.30 a.m., January 1 in the second of these—with a list of women's names, a counting of the Xmas cards. He takes an apple

> *. . . to taste the snow in it*

and thus re-enacts his father's eating of the last fruit which he sucked

> *till bright as blood the peachstone showed*
> ('Peachstone')

Life, one infers, is to be consumed, experienced until the core is what our lives leave us with. We can compose only from the stuff of our experience, feeling for roots, biting into the substance. In 'Forgotten', 'Moon object', 'An old commitment' and 'Haloes' there appears to be nothing firm, predictable, sustaining. Hearing 'Three street musicians' play the old, sentimental tunes —'The Minstrel Boy' and 'Roses of Picardy'— occasions a poignancy that raises ghosts.

Dannie Abse journeys back to Wales 'Down the M4' to visit his mother and hear the news. It is all too predictable.

Me! dutiful son going back to South Wales, this time afraid
to hear my mother's news. Too often now her friends are
    disrobed,
and my aunts and uncles, too, go into the hole, one by one.
The beautiful face of my mother is in its ninth decade.

What is to be done? With God

   further than all distance known

Dannie Abse whistles an old Yiddish tune she's taught him, but

   It won't keep.

In the fourth of these 'car journeys' he returns to London. The *abca* rhymes of the first poem in the sequence have broken into irregular rhyming in the middle two poems, but the final three lines of 'Driving home' emphasise the need for a positive act, the sense of meaning that only love can give:

 'He's waited up,' his mother says, 'to say goodnight'.
 My son smiles briefly. Such emotion! I surprise
 myself and him when I hug him tight.

As FUNLAND concludes with its long title sequence, so the section of 'New Poems '73–'76' develops the threads of wry humour and the surreal which characterised 'Funland' itself.

'Ghosts, angels, unicorns' is a performance piece in which the poet is as much concerned to exercise his wit as to exorcise any real spirits. With its side-swipes at contemporary culture—

> But the fallen dare even 10 Downing Street,
> astonish, fly through walls for their next trick;
> spotlit, enter the dreams of the important,
> slowly open their gorgeous Carnaby wings.

and the echo of a tongue-in-cheek, Larkinesque dismissal.

> No longer useful as artists' models,
> dismissed by theologians, morale tends
> to be low—even high-class angels grumble
> as they loiter in our empty churches.

Dannie Abse is having fun at our and his own expense. What significance do such things have, anyway?

> Were they the first of things to disappear
> or just mistranslations from the Hebrew?

Formal religion, he thinks, is unlikely to invoke them.

> Neutered, they hide when a gothic door opens.
> Sudden light blinds them, footsteps deafen,
> Welsh hymns stampede their shadows entirely.
> Still their stink lingers, cold stone and incense.

Ghosts, true encounters with another life, a psychic imprint beneath the surface of our day to day living, these are more likely to be experienced in the unlooked-for meeting, as with the 'Three street musicians'.

While the young, imitative Abse of AFTER EVERY GREEN THING rested on the fulsome imagery handed down from a central Christian tradition, by way of Dylan Thomas, the poetry of his sixth decade has assumed a humanist, almost anti-clerical position.

'Tales of Shatz' shows sympathy for the poetic and narrative aspects of the faith, a stoicism in the face of the great unanswered questions, the unheard prayers:

> *A certain matron of Golders Green,*
> *fingering amber beads about her neck,*
> *approaches Rabbi Shatz.*
> *When I was a small child, she thrills,*
> *once, just once, God the Holy One*
> *came through the curtains of my bedroom,*
> *What on earth has he been doing since?*

But it is a stoic resilience entrenched in language and wit, rather than justified by intervention or manifestation.

> *Rabbi Shatz turns, he squints,*
> *he stands on one leg*
> *hoping for the inspiration of a Hillel.*
> *The Holy One, he answer, blessed be He,*
> *has been waiting, waiting patiently,*
> *till you see Him again.*

Religion and poetry have at their centres a dependence on paradox; both involve a commitment to question; neither delivers easy answers.

Several of these 'New Poems '73—'76' fall short of
Dannie Abse's best work because they try to
build such easy answers—'Florida', for example,
extends a moderately good idea to breaking
point, though it can be redeemed by the poet's
lively performance at readings. 'Remembrance
Day' and 'The test', despite the skilful rhymes of
the latter, seem prosaic; at best they stretch
towards, rather than resolve observation and
feeling into fresh imagery. However, 'Cousin
Sydney' is a nicely judged piece of nostalgia, a
study in absence, and 'The silence of Tudor
Evans' is an effective short story in poem form.
With sympathy and economy this develops a
death-bed scene in which the singer and her
former professor cry, each for the other, and
themselves, while her husband remains an outsider to the last.

> *They wept together (and Tudor closed his eyes)*
> *Gwen, singer and trainer of singers*
> *because she was dying; and he, Mandlebaum,*
> *ex-physician and ex-tennis player,*
> *because he had become so ugly and so old.*

In his Gwyn Jones Lecture Dannie Abse explains
that this poem has its genesis in a Talmudic
lesson-story in which Rabbi Yohanan visits the
sick Rabbi Eliezer. He characterises this use of a
quite distinct source as the text remaining
'insoluble' in the poem. It seems that more and
more he is 'energising' his work by drawing on
traditional stories.

His latest collection of prose A STRONG DOSE OF
MYSELF has, though, two interesting additions to

the body of Abse's autobiographical fiction—'An old friend' and 'My father's red indian'. The latter probably comes as close to conventional short story form as this writer gets.

There's ample evidence in the poetry that he has a fund of stories and story-material; he shows that he can handle entirely fictional situations in his plays, and yet there is no short story in his canon, nothing that could not be read as a further chapter of his autobiography. It is intriguing to speculate how effective, say, 'The silence of Tudor Evans', might be as a short story. Or whether an earlier poem such as 'A winter convalescence' would have been a strong framing situation for its central fictional character.

The 'New Poems' section draws the COLLECTED POEMS to a close with 'The stethoscope', one of Dannie Abse's finest poems.

> *Through it,*
> *over young women's abdomens tense,*
> *I have heard the sound of creation*
> *and, in a dead man's chest, the silence*
> *before creation began.*

The questions are familiar—what exactly should he do with this stethoscope—the instrument and metonym of his professional life.

Is it to be paraded in

> *a procession of banners?*

or venerated in

> . . . *a cold, mushroom-dark church?*

Dannie Abse will never

> . . . *Mimic priest or rabbi,*
> *the swaying noises of religious men.*

He is rather a solitary celebrant—the poem is itself the act of praise and by listing an arbitrary, personal sequence of experiences he composes his own litany:

> *night cries*
> *of injured creatures, wide-eyed or blind;*
> *moonlight sonatas on a needle;*
> *lovers with doves in their throats; the wind*
> *travelling from where it began.*

These lines typify Abse at his best as a poet. Perceptive, receptive to a full range of experiences, his poetry resonates to form new imagery, to extend memory into art. The alliteration and assonance there, the para-rhyming of 'blind' and 'wind', the unnerving ambiguity of 'needle', the pacing of the final statement—there is a high degree of craft evident in that stanza, and as a conclusion the image repays the rhetoric of the second and third stanzas. He is a mature poet who has tried and mastered a number of voices, who has found his own.

Seamus Heaney, in an essay entitled 'Feeling into Words' (PREOCCUPATIONS Faber, 1980), usefully distinguishes between *Craft* and *Technique*.

104

I think technique is different from craft. Craft is what you can learn from other verse. Craft is the skill of making. It wins competitions in the IRISH TIMES or the NEW STATES-MAN. It can be deployed without reference to the feelings or the self. It knows how to keep up a capable verbal athletic display; it can be content to be 'vox et praeterea nihil'—all voice and nothing else—but not voice as in 'finding a voice'. 'Technique', as I would define it, involves not only a poet's way with words, his management of metre, rhythm and verbal texture; it involves also a definition of his stance towards life, a definition of his own reality. It involves the discovery of ways to go out of his normal cognitive bounds and raid the inarticulate: a dynamic alertness that mediates between the origins of feeling in memory and experience and the formal ploys that express these in a work of art. Technique entails the watermarking of your essential patterns of perception, voice and thought into the touch and texture of your lines; it is that whole creative effort of the mind's and body's resources to bring the meaning of experience within the jurisdiction of form. Technique is what turns, in Yeats's phrase, 'the bundle of accident and incoherence that sits down to breakfast' into 'an idea, something intended, complete'.

I think that in the mature work of Dannie Abse we witness serious and convincing evidence of a poet bringing 'the meaning of experience within the jurisdiction of form'. His latest collection proclaims him to be both 'Way out' and 'In the centre'. I do not think that this is to be read as an admission of confusion in the sense of a weakness. Dannie Abse is a poet who feeds off that basic sense of ambiguity and several sets of contradictions.

The title of his collection WAY OUT IN THE CENTRE is taken from the closing line of the poem 'A note to Donald Davie in Tennessee'. There is of course a pun on the Americanism of the 1960s in 'way out'. Dannie Abse is aware of the eminently respected positions held by established literary figures such as Davie and himself, but is constantly reminded of their common mortality and the dangerous position which any serious poet must assume: he is 'dangerous' both in a social and emotional sense.

Dannie Abse's 'technique' embodies that questioning uncertainty of a self-confessed

> *reluctant puritan*

His poetry is shot through with concern. It is also propelled by a craft that is skilled in prosody. It ranges in his latest work from the free verse of 'Orpheus in the surgery' and 'Bedtime story' to the *aba* rhymes of 'A winter visit' and 'X-ray'. He affectionately mimics William Carlos Williams's 'The Term' in 'A London street scene' and reworks Chasidic stories in 'Of Rabbi Yose', 'Snake' and 'Of Itzig and his dog'.

His mastery of the poet's craft gives him a range of inflexions and moods. He talks specifically of one new poem from this collection in his essay 'On Rhyming and Not Rhyming' (A STRONG DOSE OF MYSELF p. 166.) He reveals that the genesis of 'In the gallery' was a rhyming couplet—

> *Think blue, say green,*
> *squeeze apple-pips from a tangerine.*

106

which came to him during a question and answer session following a poetry reading. This seemingly gratuitous rhyme became linked to another apparently random response to a scene of birds rising out of snow on a television programme—

> Four hoofmarks in the snow
> flew away. They must have been four crows.

In successive drafts the original couplet lost its place in the order of things and the second couplet evolves a more effective shape. That story has a fitting quality when one considers that the finished poem is essentially about deception, about the illusion of form and structure, in art just as in our everyday perceptions. A poem which begins in a craft workshop manner develops, through the 'small surprises' that crafting skill creates, into another manifestation of the poet's 'technique'. Dannie Abse is intrigued by that fourth crow: it is central to his purpose that the seeds of uncertainty lodge in our memory of the scene.

WAY OUT IN THE CENTRE has a body of poems which confirms an established writer in his maturity, rather than pointing to radical developments in either his style or subject-matter. The opening poem, 'Smile Please', is another look at 'Epithalamion' and with the poem that follows, 'Bedtime story', Dannie Abse continues the theme of 'Ghosts, angels, unicorns' from the COLLECTED POEMS. As in 'The test', where Nell Gwyn was metamorphosed, Abse sees how a 'derelict' might be perceived as 'the wrong Mary'. The poet is 'a fortunate man', but all around him are

> . . . *unfortunate creatures, angels botched*

whose leader

> . . . *stands motionless in long black overcoat*
> *on spoiled snow* . . .

It has the disturbing effect of cinema—Strelnikov staring out from the rear of the train across the snow in DOCTOR ZHIVAGO.

Again, 'Night village' transforms the banalities of a night drive into the surreal images of nightmare; and 'The empty building at night' jolts the poet making his way home after work across the city. An emptiness, a social guilt aches in him as he looks up

> . . . *to see alas what I knew I would: the wakeful*
> *moon too near.*

In the centre of things, in middle-age, in London, in the literary scene, Dannie Abse travels imaginatively 'way out'.

As a doctor he strains to re-assure, to be professional, to offer the security, the rational diagnosis and prescription. Yet he is constantly addressing the issue raised by Philip Larkin's question in 'Days':

> *Where can we live but days?*
>
> *Ah, solving that question*
> *Brings the priest and the doctor*
> *In their long coats*
> *Running over the fields.*

Dannie Abse feels at times that the purple cloak may be as efficacious as the white coat. 'The doctor', as well as re-iterating the duality of his own roles, reflects that crisis of confidence in their rational training that takes more and more practitioners beyond the conventions of their field.

> *So the doctor will and yes he will prescribe*
> *the usual dew from a banana leaf; poppies and*
> *honey too; ten snowflakes or something whiter*
> *from the bole of a tree; the clearest water*
> *ever, melting ice from a mountain lake;*
> *sunlight from waterfall's edge, rainbow smoke;*
> *tears from eyelashes of the daughter.*

There is no cure for the human condition: we answer our fate with our emotions—words and gestures, feelings and actions.

With characteristic black humour in 'Pantomime diseases' the poet dismisses the fairy-tale world of passive innocence.

> *When the three Darling children thought they'd fly*
> *to Never-Never Land—the usual trip—*
> *their pinpoint pupils betrayed addiction.*
> *And not hooked by Captain Hook but by*
> *that ponce, Peter Pan. All the rest is fiction.*

This is a marvellous performance piece, grouchy and biting in its wit. But the most enduring poems in this book are, appropriately, the two in memory of his mother—'A winter visit' and 'X-ray', and then the closing poem, 'Last words'.

109

In 'A winter visit', again he is confronted by the frailty, the inevitably close death of a parent. Feeling the oncoming tears, he calls on his professional reserve:

> *Yet must not (although only Nothing keeps)*
> *for I inhabit a white coat not a black*
> *even here—and am not qualified to weep.*

and resolves his dilemma through an image arising from anecdote.

> *So I speak of small approximate things,*
> *of how I saw, in the park, four flamingoes*
> *standing, one-legged on ice, heads beneath wings.*

This is Abse's strength: to reclaim, like a painter's pentimenti, the significance of shapes beneath the surface. The flamingoes, irrational, apparently unrelated as pentimenti beneath a finished oil-painting, have a poignant and entirely appropriate sadness in the context of the poem.

His practised skill in the chest clinic is now an acute burden in 'X-ray'. At such moments the doctor want to suppress his learning.

> *As a boy it was so: you know how*
> *my small hand never teased to pieces*
> *an alarm clock or flensed a perished mouse.*

> *And this larger hand's the same. It stretches now*
> *out from a white sleeve to hold up, mother,*
> *your X-ray to the glowing screen. My eyes look*
> *but don't want to; I still don't want to know.*

So many poems are hung between the white coat and the purple cloak. The structuring of these medical poems in the collection underlines the impression that Dannie Abse wishes to make: 'A winter visit' and 'X-ray' are held apart by 'The doctor', whilst 'Pantomime diseases' closes the group and precedes the three poems from Yiddish sources and the four transpositions from other cultures and languages.

'Lunch and afterwards' launches from the personal tragedy of 'X-ray' into a bizarre image occasioned by a pathologist's remark over lunch.

> *'After death, of all soft tissues the brain's*
> *the first to vanish, the uterus the last.'*

Afterwards, finding himself alone in his house, Dannie Abse has a powerful sense of loneliness and despair. He reacts irrationally, as if to break the spell of gloom.

> *I stood next to the telephone*
> *I thought of a number doubled it.*

This second part of 'No reply' is a long set of unpunctuated statements contrasting with the three-line verses of 'Lunch with the pathologist.' The effect is cumulative; it seems that the climax is reached inevitably, no matter how odd the act might appear.

The final poem in the collection is, just as appropriately, a tightly structured piece—five line-stanzas, the second and fifth lines rhyming and each stanza pressed from the same syllabic template. With 'Last words' Dannie Abse seems to be aiming at the same target as in 'Pantomime diseases'—the 'quotable fictions' by which we salve our fears about trauma and death. Yet, whilst seeing through the actors' 'pithy pretences', he has to confess that such brave gestures may be the most natural, affirmative human response to our leaving this earth.

> *Death scenes not life-enhancing,*
> *death scenes not beautiful nor with breeding;*
> *yet bravo Sydney Carton, bravo Duc de Chavost*
> *who, euphoric beside the guillotine, turned down*
> *the corner of the page he was reading.*

The most fitting last scene for Dannie Abse would be a private one, fingers touching out language to the last:

> *but finger-tapping still our private morse, '. . . love you,'*
> *before the last flowers and flies descend.*

Over the last forty years Dannie Abse has produced a body of work—fiction, autobiography, drama, criticism and poetry—which should claim an important place for him in post-war British literature. Two books—ASH ON A YOUNG MAN'S SLEEVE and the COLLECTED POEMS—separated by a quarter of a century, have to be considered in any serious attempt to assess writing in Britain in the second half of this century. The range and consistency of his prose work offer insights into the nature of the poet's calling and practice which are of real value and are, moreover, always entertaining and accessible.

His contribution to the literature of Wales is major—by the example of his books and by a continuing loyalty to Cardiff and the land of his birth. There is an irony here in that, as the self-proclaimed 'outsider', Dannie Abse has the nostalgic attachment to Wales that is at the heart of so many of those outside the Welsh language who feel that they too are truly Welsh.

Appearing in an episode of David Smith's television series WALES! WALES? (1/4/84, BBC 2) the poet was shown driving back to Wales down the motorway. He was heard reading 'Down the M4', which was followed by the statements:

I think of Wales as my wife and London as my mistress.
I think of Wales as certain details of Cardiff and
where we are now in Ogmore-by-Sea.

Also Dannie Abse is representative of the professional in a technological world who is profoundly disturbed by and suspicious of that modern world; someone who finds himself turning to explore alternative and more traditional stories and models for his writing.

The man who is 'way out' in his dedication to writing is undeniably in touch with 'the centre'. He has recently explained his position as a writer:

I am committed to the next poem that 'happens' and then the next. I say 'happens' because I have never been able to will a poem into existence. Though poetry is written in the brain the brain is bathed in blood, and consequently one must wait for —to use an old-fashioned word—'inspiration'. Sometimes whilst waiting I have written novels and plays, for I would rather write, say, a play, than commit fine thoughts to a note-book or private diary. In any case, as I grow older, my thinking becomes more confused. I mean that the more I read and the more I experience and the more I know, the more I journey into ignorance.

I am still waiting for the next poem, and if the periods of waiting sometimes become prolonged, I recall my motto, which is: 'Be visited, expect nothing, and endure.'

It is that sense of expectancy, when, as Renée Winegarten has noted, *uninvited ghosts stalk through his poems*, which draws us back again and again to his best poems. These represent experiences in which we *cannot quite touch bottom*, and because of that quality Dannie Abse's work celebrates the fact of our shared living, affirming that we are all held in the exciting predicament between under-standing and mystery.

Bibliography

DANNIE ABSE

AFTER EVERY GREEN THING, Hutchinson &
Co., London, 1948.

WALKING UNDER WATER, Hutchinson & Co.,
London, 1952.

ASH ON A YOUNG MAN'S SLEEVE, Hutchinson
& Co., London, 1954; Criterion Books, New York,
1955, Second English edition: Pergamon Press
Ltd., Oxford, 1969; Third edition: Valentine,
Mitchell & Co., London, 1971, 1973; Fourth
edition: Corgi Books, London, 1972; Fifth edition:
Penguin Books Ltd., London, 1982, reprinted 1983.

SOME CORNER OF AN ENGLISH FIELD,
Hutchinson & Co., London, 1956; Criterion
Books, New York, 1956.

TENANTS OF THE HOUSE: POEMS 1951–1956,
Hutchinson & Co., London, 1957; reprinted 1958;
Criterion Books, New York, 1959.

POEMS, GOLDERS GREEN, Hutchinson & Co.,
London, 1962.

THREE QUESTOR PLAYS, Scorpion Press,
London, 1967.

115

MEDICINE ON TRIAL, Aldus Books, London, 1967; reprinted Crown Publishers, New York, 1969.

A SMALL DESPERATION, Hutchinson & Co., London, 1968.

O. JONES, O. JONES, Hutchinson & Co., London, 1970.

SELECTED POEMS, Hutchinson & Co., London, 1970; reprinted 1971 and 1973; Oxford University Press, New York, 1970.

FUNLAND AND OTHER POEMS, Hutchinson & Co., London, 1973; reprinted 1974; Oxford University Press, New York, 1973.

THE DOGS OF PAVLOV, Valentine, Mitchell & Co., London, 1973.

A POET IN THE FAMILY, Hutchinson & Co., London, 1974.

COLLECTED POEMS 1948–1976, Hutchinson & Co., London, 1977; reprinted 1981; University of Pittsburgh Press, Pittsburgh, 1977.

PYTHAGORAS, Hutchinson & Co., London, 1979.

MISCELLANY ONE, Poetry Wales Press, Bridgend, 1981.

WAY OUT IN THE CENTRE, Hutchinson & Co., London, 1981; reprinted as ONE LEGGED ON

ICE, University of Georgia Press, Athens, Georgia, 1983.

A STRONG DOSE OF MYSELF, Hutchinson & Co., 1983.

THE GWYN JONES LECTURE, 1984, 'Under the influence of,' University College of Wales, Cardiff.

Works Edited by Dannie Abse

POETRY AND POVERTY, Nos. 1–7, ed. Dannie Abse, London, 1949–1954; reprinted by Kraus Thomson Organisations Ltd., Nendeln, Leichtenstein, 1968.

MAVERICKS, eds. Dannie Abse and Howard Sergeant, Editions Poetry and Poverty, London, 1957.

MODERN EUROPEAN VERSE. THE POCKET POETS, ed. Dannie Abse, Corgi Books, London, 1971–1973.

POETRY DIMENSION ANNUAL, Nos. 2–7, ed. Dannie Abse, Robson Books Ltd., London, 1974–1980.

MY MEDICAL SCHOOL, ed. Dannie Abse, Robson Books Ltd., London, 1978.

WALES IN VERSE, ed. Dannie Abse, Secker and Warburg, London, 1983.

DOCTORS AND PATIENTS, ed. Dannie Abse, Oxford University Press, London, 1984.

Criticism on the Work of Dannie Abse

THE POETRY OF DANNIE ABSE – Critical Essays and Reminiscences edited by Joseph Cohen, Robson Books, London, 1983.

Other Critical Essays

Roland Mathias, 'The Head Still Stuffed with Feathers', THE ANGLO-WELSH REVIEW, Vol. 15 No. 36, Summer 1966.

John Smith, 'The Search for Identity'. CAHIERS FRANCO-ANGLAIS, No. 1, POESIE VIVANTE, 1967.

Roland Mathias, 'The One Voice That is Mine', THE ANGLO-WELSH REVIEW, Vol. 16 No. 38, Winter 1967.

Jeremy Robson, 'Dannie Abse', CORGI MODERN POETS IN FOCUS No. 4, 1971.

John Pikoulis, 'Predicaments of Otherness', POETRY WALES, Vol. 13 No. 2, 1977.

John Tripp, 'Dannie Abse Revisited', POETRY WALES, Vol. 13 No. 2, October 1977.

Fleur Adcock, 'Poet on Poet', AMBIT No. 70, 1977.

Howard Sergeant, 'The Poetry of Dannie Abse', BOOKS AND BOOKMEN, July 1977.

David Punter, 'Varieties of Defiance', STRAIGHT LINES No. 2, 1979.

Glyn Jones, 'Dannie Abse' in PROFILES, Gomer Press, Llandysul, 1980.

Renée Winegarten, 'Dannie Abse: Vision and Reality', JEWISH CHRONICLE LITERARY SUPPLEMENT, 24 Dec. 1982.

Daniel Hoffman, 'Doctor and Magus in the Work of Dannie Abse', LITERATURE AND MEDICINE, No. 3, 1984.

J. P. Ward, 'Science Poetry: Approaches to Redgrove, Abse and Ammons', POESIS, 1984.

William Oxley, THE INNER TAPESTRY, The University of Salzburg Press, Germany, 1984.

The Author

Tony Curtis was born in Carmarthen in 1946. He went to Queen Elizabeth Grammar School, Carmarthen, and to Greenhill School, Tenby. He read English at Swansea University and, more recently, took a Master's degree in Creative Writing at Goddard College, Vermont.

He has published three collections of poetry— ALBUM, PREPARATIONS and LETTING GO—and has edited PEMBROKESHIRE POEMS, THE ART OF SEAMUS HEANEY and WALES: THE IMAGINED NATION. He was elected as a member of the Welsh Academy in 1976 and served as its Chairman in 1984–85. He received an Eric Gregory Award for his poetry in 1972, the Welsh Arts Council's Young Poets Prize in 1974, and in 1984 he was the winner of the National Poetry Competition. He is Senior Lecturer in English at the Polytechnic of Wales and lives in Barry with his wife and two children.

Acknowledgement

I wish to thank Dr Glyn Jones who read the typescript and made valuable suggestions; and Margaret Curtis, Michael Parnell and Peter Wilson for their reading of the book in its later stages. Their reactions were very helpful, though they are not to be blamed for any inaccuracies or shortcomings which may remain.

*This Edition
designed by Jeff Clements
is set in Monotype Spectrum 12 Didot on 13 points
and printed on Basingwerk Parchment by
Qualitex Printing Limited, Cardiff*

It is limited to 1000 copies of which this is

Copy No. 0527

British Library Cataloguing in Publication Data

Curtis, Tony
    Dannie Abse.—(Writers of Wales, ISSN 0141–5050)
    1. Abse, Dannie—Biography   2. Poets, Welsh—
    20th Century—Biography
    I. Title   II. Series
    821′.914   PR6001.B7Z/
    ISBN 0–7083–0896–1